It's Not Even the Gist

For the world.

Contents:

Preface

I'm twenty-two years old. I started drinking when I was thirteen, and quit when I was twenty. I used a slew of drugs, illicit and prescription. But my life consists of more than just that. Currently, my face-blindness and sensory disorder leave me in a lost and confused state, but I manage to get by. I've broken up my life with black-outs and memory loss. The memories I do have are often stark, vivid and burdensome. I thought I'd alleviate some of that weight by writing this book. I hope you enjoy it, for then there will be some use for all that I have felt.

Holidays

Growing up I didn't celebrate Halloween. I personally found it silly and labor intensive; all the decorating and dressing up. It would be cheaper and simpler to just buy candy. I didn't see the point. My family didn't celebrate, because it was pagan, or in other words evil and ungodly. So we'd shut our lights off and send all the children away.

When I was newly enrolled in public school rather than being homeschooled, more open to the world, a freer spirit, I went trick-or-treating with a couple of my friends. I was probably ten. I didn't have or make a costume, I just wore my leotard and tights from gymnastics class, so I was a "gymnast." My one friend said she was going to be a "star," but ended up just painting her whole self pitch-black with body paint. She wore regular clothes. I don't remember what my other friend went as, maybe a clown or something.

It was us three girls, my friend's mom and the mom's boyfriend. We rode in his truck to the nicer neighborhoods. Big houses, better candy. Almost each house, we egged after we left. My "star" friend was getting body paint all over, on everything she touched and brushed against— including the beautiful houses.

We all had pillowcases except the adults. They were heavy with candy and objects. The mom was the most enthusiastic about stealing lawn ornaments and halloween decorations. "Here! Isn't that cute?" I'd stuff it in with my candy. We stole pumpkins, jack-o-lanterns, fake spiders, little scarecrows. We hurled eggs over lawns and scurried back to the truck to continue our escapade elsewhere.

When we got back to my friend's house, late, the mom pointed to the empty steps of the porch. She spoke with a smile."Look, someone got our pumpkins too!"

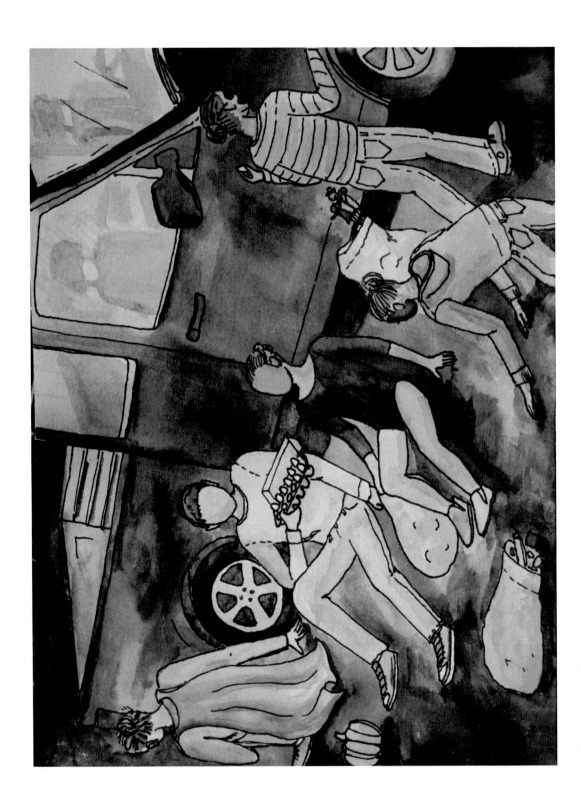

Wrong House

I stayed the night at a friend's house, and was brushing my teeth at six-something in the morning, trying to convince myself to wait to drink. I had a gatorade bottle in my bag full of vodka. I was chugging it by seven am. I blacked out. I was face down, hussing and fussing in my friend's arms, and she was asking if I wanted her to stay with me. She was maybe five years older than me. I might have been thirteen. She left with her family to go camping and I slept it off in the empty house. When I woke up I called someone to pick me up and I went outside to wait. I was hungover, not sure who saw what or where everyone went. I was walking up the road because I hated to stay still, and realized I forgot my bible.

I went back into the house, through the garage, and through the unlocked door. A large, wriggly, fluffy dog greeted me. "Aw, I didn't know you guys had a dog!" I said. I pet it, and there was an older white man in his underwear at the table, watching tube television and eating cereal. "I just came back to get my book," I informed him genuinely. He just kinda looked at me as he chewed and swallowed. I must have walked almost into the other room and then blurted out "I'm in the wrong house." The man laughed fully as I exited the abode. He didn't even seem to mind, and I went into the house I was supposed to, then went back outside to catch my ride.

Hoppin'

Used to pool-hop. Run through people's back yards, careen myself over the edges of pools, or slip into the below-ground ones. One day we had the balls to go during the day, my friend and I. He was pretty reserved; played videogames and slept a lot. He had never had a drink before.

It was an in-ground pool with a couple of coolers full of alcohol and a panel wooden fence. We swam for maybe three hours, quiet and cautious at first, but then running and jumping. Trying to stand up on the floaties.

I had started with the liquor and the real beer. It was more than a jackpot. I eventually convinced the kid to drink the hard lemonade kind. He said it tasted like a Jolly Rancher. I'm pretty sure the shit was pink.

Eventually the owner came home. Our pasty asses must have had sunburns by then. The back sliding-glass-door slid open and a head popped out. "Are you done?" I replied with a "yes" and my friend hopped the fence. Dripping wet I filled my arms with liquor and lawn ornaments. "Take these!" I was handing them over the fence and then I jumped over. We ran, hands full of goodies, and we dodged traffic and changed up our route since the owner of the house was chasing us in a Camaro. We got on the bus.

Pseudo-grandma

My pseudograndmother is a regular character to me in my life. But there was something alluring about her. She threw her hands up one day and said "That's it! I'm done with this cat! He just peed in my purse!" They actually got rid of him.

We as a family took turns sleeping all together in her bed at night. I don't know why. Because it was the most comfortable bed, maybe, and it was spacious. She had the master bedroom in this big col de sac house that was out of context from the rest of my life. My "sister" and I would fight each other and push each other down the stairs, fighting our way up to her bathroom whenever we had to shit at the same time. The downstairs bathroom was clogged by anything other than air, and the normal bathroom was typically coated with hair and urine. I remember the content look of her entity when she won and I'd have to hold mine in.

There was a solace to that master space. Airy and lightly colored, there was a vanity, a bed, and a 19" television on a little stand. We would watch what I think were sitcoms or something from all the way across the room. We'd sit in the bed, me and my "grandmother," her in her underwear with a bottle of wine. I couldn't even see what was on the TV. It was so far away.

She had this weighted hula hoop, with some padding on it that she would swing 'round her nearly bare hips in the empty space of the room. She certainly gave that room life. I tried using the hoop once, and my hips were bruised badly for a week. I think that underneath the padding, it was made of metal. She could hula for what seemed like an endless forty-five minutes. But maybe it was only ten.

Last time I saw her, I entered her room with her grandson in an apartment. She was lying down in bed and he said "Do it! Do it! Dab!" She swung her head into the crook of her arm with her other arm extended out. She hadn't sat up to do it. She laughed. "You're welcome to visit anytime!"

Sometimes There

I drank a lot of Robitussin as a kid. I'd snort Sudafed until I'd pass out. Clear water would run out of my nose. In middle school I started drinking and smoking pot. I much preferred the alcohol. I blacked out the first time I drank.

In my middle school days I counted Wednesdays as bonus Fridays. So I'd only partake in "partying" a couple times a week. There was a thrill and a relief in it, like I was the boss of what I was doing and feeling. In reality it was the loss of control I was begging for. I didn't want to be so aware, or experience this life anymore. Blacking out was my way of leaving without leaving. Throughout my drinking career, so many people didn't even know I was gone.

In highschool I drank more weekdays. I went to college parties and nonchalantly drank other people's beer. I was fourteen at a party when a sixteen-year-old girl (we were the youngest ones there) sat by me. "Hey, we have the same drink!" I said yeah, we do. Later she came back to me. "You drank my beer, you bitch." I didn't care. People would make up stories about me, like how I was the tag-along kid who gave blow-jobs. I'd drink until the next place sounded more appealing. Often somewhere that had liquor.

By tenth-grade I was drinking all day every day. I'd leave the house between one and three in the morning on my bicycle. I'd go into Hannaford with an empty book-bag and place two six-packs in it, stacked on top of each other. I'd zip it up and walk out. I'd place the beer somewhere in the brush, and ride another mile to

Price Chopper. I could often cram a twelve-pack of bottles into the bag. So when I arrived back at the other beer, I'd swap the six-packs out for the twelve. I'd leave with the six-packs on my back and the twelve-pack balanced on my knee. I'd pedal home. I typically did this twice a week. I took canned beer out of the fridge from my mother, wine from my step-father, liquor from next door and home, if my mom had any vodka. I put Four Locos in my sweatshirt at gas stations, propping them up with my hand in my pocket as a shelf. I'd also get alcohol from anyone who would share, or give into my pleas. Sometimes I was lucky and the coolers on the brims of houses had abandoned drinks in them.

I'd drink first thing in the morning. I'd put six beers, if not more, in my book-bag amongst my papers. I filled Gatorade bottles with wine lightened in color by vodka. My water bottles I'd set right on my desk. My Poland Spring was really tequila.

I'd be shaking and squirming in chemistry class. Every day I would try to make it past second period without a drink. I don't believe I ever made it. I'd bring my stash and drink, sitting on the toilet in the bathroom. I bent the caps off with my teeth, and I'd put the remaining beer (if I had any) in a Mountain Dew bottle.

There was this joke going around, where people would empty someone's book-bag, turn it inside out, put the materials back in and zip it up like that. They called it "sacking." The owner of the bag would come back, and everyone would laugh. Sometimes my drunk self would leave my bag, but before I left I'd look at the class and say "if you touch my bag, I'll kill you." No one ever went in it.

Tenth-grade was a brown-out. I used to punch this kid in the back of the head in english class. I was yelling one day during a test and the teacher came over to my desk. "I totally agree with you, but you're going to have to go." She was writing a hall pass for me to go to an office— I don't know which one.

"Nice bottle opener." I had placed my keys on the desk and sat on my leg. "It's not a bottle opener." "Yes it is." "No, it's a metal brace, for broken wood. I got it from my dad." It was a mending brace, and looked kind of like that thing that goes around the latch-hole for a door, but was pristinely rectangular. "It's a bottle opener." That *is* what I used it for, but I argued with my spanish teacher about it. I faded into somebody braiding my hair, and I was talking, in that same class. I was often black-out drunk by then. Sometimes I would go to the teachers the next day and apologize. "What's up with you?" Or else they would turn their heads away.

I volunteered at a church up the street from my house and would show up drunk. I'd sneak outside into the bushes to drink the beer I'd hidden, through a straw. Then I'd go into the bathroom and thoroughly wash my mouth out with soap. *Then they won't smell it.* That's what the straw was for, too. I'd drink the alcohol directly into my throat. Nobody knew for a while, but my behavior got worse. I remember restraining a younger kid and asking him repeatedly what the problem was. He eventually scampered out of my hold. I let him go. I'd be lying on the floor, room spinning from alcohol and cough syrup. One day I was hiding under the desk in an empty office. A church leader came in and leaned over to look. "Boo!" I put my hands up, smiling. That's when he stood straight up and said "That's enough."

The church wanted to get a hold of my mom, so I had my friend call them. "Hi, this is Leah's mom. You wanted to talk to me? Here's my number." The church called back after receiving the message. "Hello? Who? This is Erica." The leaders came back to me. "Nice try." They eventually got me set up with outpatient rehab.

When my mom found out I was drinking, she took my stash of fifty-plus beers and started drinking them herself. "Mm... this is good." I stood tense in the doorway. I was internally flighty but held incredibly still, and silent. She just looked at me, my beer in her hand. "How could you do this?"

I started hiding my beer better. Liquor in little decorative containers around my room. One day I didn't have enough, and it was time for school. I walked in the opposite direction, two miles. I stepped into a gas station and the clerk was bent down behind the counter. Cigarettes or something. I snatched the alcohol closest to the door— a twelve pack of Bud Light. I ran out and into the woods. *I know these woods.* But I wasn't where I thought I was. The brush was thick and trip-and-fall inducing. I took my sweatshirt off and draped it over the box of beer like a tarp, so no one would see what it was. I walked back out to the road, ashamed of my stealth, and muddy. "Ya know that's my property." A man was looking up from a car he was working on, I think. "Sorry. I wasn't doing anything illegal." "Like what?" "I don't know. Airsoft?" I walked back towards the school, drinking some on the way and placing the rest of the beers in my sweatshirt like a satchel. I might have stopped home.

I'm sitting in a conference room at Schenectady High School, almost all the guidance counselors, principals, whatever, sitting around the table and looking at me. "I'm not even drunk! I only had like ten drinks!" It was about eleven o'clock in the morning.*Khhertt* "We found another can crumpled in a feminine disposal container in the bathroom. Bud Light." "That's not mine!" I don't know what happened after that.

Piece of Cake

I remember chillin' in a rickety upstairs apartment with my friends and the foster kids. We were all sort of mixed-in. It was one of the mom's birthday, and we were all pretty poor.

One of the moms, a forty-year-old redheaded horse farmer I was slightly in love with, was dumping out her purse onto the floor. Fondling the dirty change, they were trying to scrounge up enough for a cake. It was a group effort. I put my only ten dollars on the floor. It was rare that I had cash. I'm the girl who shoplifted beer and stole a bra that would fit me and proceeded to wear it three whole years.

We bought a cake and gathered, crammed like old dust in the living room. The floor creaked as we sang happy birthday and the guy carrying the cake tripped over the edge of the couch. We were singing "to you…" as the cake flipped and smeared frosting-first across the floor, and that surface was by no means clean enough to eat off of.

Onset

When I got to the end of tenth-grade, I had been admitted to outpatient rehabilitation treatment. I still drank, but less, and swallowed white vinegar to help me pass the piss-tests. I started running track in school, so I moved my drinking to just mornings. Having beer in my stomach during practice didn't feel so good. I'd run on some afternoons to treatment, instead of with the team. Once, as we were doing high-knees for warm-up, the coach said we should be drinking sixteen ounces of water first thing in the morning. She held up her hands to show how much. I thought to myself, that's how much beer I drink before I get on the bus.

As the season went on, I actually got sober. I switched from self-medicating with alcohol to running and losing weight. As I got better at running, I ran more and ate less. I'd walk or run instead of riding the school-bus, and I'd eat very little throughout the day. I got thinner. I became tired. I was always cold. My eyes became real sensitive to light, so I'd wear sunglasses all day to accent my constantly-worn peacoat. One teacher used to grab the lapels of my jacket and shake them in her fists. "You're so cute! I just want to take you home." I sometimes wondered if she would.

I slept through all my classes, earning only attendance, and I'd wake up to run at track practice after school. One day, I told the security officer that my toes were numb. Two days later, the numbness had moved up through my whole body, my face, and even down my throat. The security officer brought me to the social worker who brought me home. She looked at my mom. "Bring her to the emergency room right now." She thought I was having a stroke. I wasn't very responsive in those days.

They did some bloodwork and sent me home with the diagnosis of mononucleosis. As the days went by, my health got worse. The numbness had turned into burning pain. I had to wear a certain type of dress pant as to not aggravate my legs. I had to pull my upper legs forward to walk. My feet dragged. The currents of pain in my legs started when I was running indoor track. The day after sectionals, I squirmed in the fleece sheets and blankets that couldn't keep me warm, with a migraine and those thick currents of pain that flowed up and down my legs.

We ended up back at the doctor's multiple times, my mom getting into fights with them about there being something wrong. They insisted it was just mono, that I'd feel like crap from four to eight months and get over it. I couldn't fathom being sick for that long. What about track? That's how I stayed sober. It had become something important to me. It was one of the only things I did anymore besides walk, paint, sleep, and loathe myself. I'd sit at the table, looking over a cup of coffee, and hate myself.

Eventually I was referred to neurology. A hyper little Mexican man was my doctor. He listened to us, and was kind. He prescribed me gabapentin and it helped with the pain. He ordered an MRI, a spinal tap, and a nerve-conduction test. As he put the tiny needles into my numb legs, I barely felt the shocks. I didn't know they *were* shocks. They felt like vibrations. "I'm good?" "Mm... well, you're not normal." I took it as a jest, but he was being serious. I ignored the idea of it mattering.

He came back with the diagnosis of Chronic Inflammatory Demyelinating Polyradiculoneuropathy. He tipped his head, little nod. "It's polyradiculous." I might have replied with a laugh. He explained to me what it meant. "Chronic is a long time, inflammatory means the nerves are inflamed, demyelinating means the protective coating that directs nerve signals is being eaten off of your nerves, poly means all over, radiculo means the nerve damage originates from the bottom of your spine, and neuropathy is the pain. The burning. The shocking pains."

I stayed home from school for some months and slowly omitted each thing I enjoyed. I had quit drinking, cut out sugar, stopped watching movies and reading, didn't listen to music. I didn't even paint. I was doing a morbid buddhist thing. I sat in the yard with my dog. Then stood up. Then sat down. Then stood up again. I was uncomfortable, and my spine hurt tremendously.

I got to the point of starvation and nothingness. I was hospitalized. I had a near-death experience and ended up walking with a walker after being acutely paralyzed. I remember the first tense burning steps I took across the kitchen floor. I couldn't see, for a day or two. My vision and hearing slowly came back. At first, I had pinhole vision and became obsessed with taking pictures. The small area of them was easier for me to see. I thought I wanted to be alive, and I started talking to everyone. I still had to wear sunglasses to look at my phone screen. I felt and heard the grinding of the bones in my neck. I was so thin I could barely hold my head up. I'd have to lie very still, at times, and let my spine's throbbing die down before I was permitted to move again. I slowly regained health, ate lots of protein. But the pain didn't go away. I pushed through anyways. I figured I should get used to life this way, it being chronic.

In the summer between my junior and senior year, I started running again. I ran with some coaches and long-distance runners through the trails in the park. We upped my meds. One day I was talking to a bulky coach. "I have a neurological disorder." "Oh, that's why you fall all the time." That felt like a tinge of a reality check. I thought I fell just as much as anyone else who tripped over a stick or a root. I do recall motioning people to go past me, because my legs didn't work to get up right away.

Inside school I'd fall a lot in the hallways. The security officer would move me to the edge of the walkways and the guidance counselors would ask me where my Life Alert button was. "I've fallen and I can't get up!" I'd fall and trip, leaning and pushing against the walls all the way down the hall to get outside for cross-country practice. I'd thrust myself forward and out of the building by the doorjambs to run. Once I'd get moving into a stride, I wouldn't fall. If I took my meds too close to practice, I'd throw them up. "I threw up my pills, I'll be in more pain today." My coach would just say OK.

After races and the faster pacing at the end, I'd take a few steps and often fall. My legs would give up on me for a while. One day I dragged myself on my knees over to my coach. "I can't walk." "Alright, go ahead and get on the bus."

Dead Weight

The first time I was paralyzed was shortly after being discharged from the hospital. The nutritionist hadn't cleared me, but she wasn't on shift and the doctors came into my room. People had been visiting and bringing me things. I was wearing a kool-aid t-shirt and there were flowers, books and an old origami paper calendar. The one doctor with large hands he often clasped together looked at a plastic dinosaur with a straw for a tail and said sideways: You can't live here.

I guess I seemed too happy to be in the hospital. I couldn't digest my food. I was close to enlightenment. I was anorexic and everyone at school could tell. My infusion nurse insisted that it was important, that I had to tell my mom. My mom was advocating for a feeding tube and so was I but what I really meant was just vitamins. I couldn't think clearly, and my mom was yelling about me catching anorexia from a viral infection. I think she realized the gravity of something as she slid to the floor and held her hand to her head in the emergency room. I wish I could feel appropriate emotions for that.

I argued a little with the doctors and insisted that the nutritionist had to check in with me tomorrow. They said "you have a place to go." I froze in response because I couldn't articulate that I didn't. My home environment was my self-destructing ring.

My mom threw the hospital pillows in the car and the tech that had wheeled me out sort of smiled. "After all that shit, I'm takin' these!" She slammed the door.

I was always cushioned up since my bones were poking out. Wasn't my idea. My nurse had me sit on a pillow in the car and asked "Are you always like this?" I was always bracing myself, trying to relieve the pressure. My social worker came into my sunny backyard one day and asked if I knew why I was in pain. "Your bones are pressing through your skin." I didn't answer.

The large-mitted doctor had laughed when he saw how many pillows I slept on. "I have to." I remember the nurse helping me with my blankets. I couldn't even put up my own hair. "Are you comfortable?" Then my reigning truth came out then, at sixteen-years old. "I'm never comfortable."

We stopped at Stewart's and I was in mania. I exclaimed that I didn't give a fuck. I ate a whole ice cream cone with sprinkles in a bowl since I couldn't manipulate eating without getting it all over myself. My body didn't take to it at all and my urine was thick like milk. I didn't sweat anymore, and otherwise everything was discolored.

In my bedroom there was light, splatter paint, many pictures, and the visuals were all too overwhelming. I had to walk all the way to the kitchen to get my pills. That was maybe ten feet away, but it was more than I moved in the hospital. I was severely over-stimulated. After I took the meds if I even got to reaching the cupboard, I went to the living room for the phone and called my mom. I wasn't going to make it. "Do you want me to come home between shifts? Do you want me to come home between shifts? Leah?"

I was down on the floor, the phone somewhere, my hair out, sprawled like it had never been, and my mom was pulling in the gravel driveway. My brother was in the kitchen, pouring cereal as he heard the car. I could see the car. I could see myself, face-down on the floor. I could see my mom from above her head. My brother shoved the bag of cereal down into the box and ran away. I saw him scurrying and slurping the cereal down the hall. He was older than me. We all have anxiety. It was simultaneous and I saw it in slow-motion. Her reaching for the doorknob, me still on the floor, my brother staccato-running. I heard the keys jingle. Back to silence, or at least to regular noise. "I can't move!" Is what I said at some point, I think. My brother and my mom lifted me by the armpits and dragged me to the bedroom before mine. I was crying, and my brother had no idea what was going on. We lived in the same house but barely saw each other. My mom had beckoned him out of his room.

I was put on the bed and the door was shut. It was dark; a reprieve. The walls were darker and covered in staples. The curtains were a dark navy-blue. The sun came in, more as a shadow than a warmth. I think I died. I had an overwhelming noise fill what I can't even comprehend. I saw myself lying in the bed and all my skin started to come off. It happened to be in more colors than I'd ever seen, and the shreds of skin were sucked up in a whirlwind; more skin than I ever thought I had. It all disappeared into the ceiling and I was gone. Not my body, just me.

Flooded Homeopathy

I was riding my bike through a flood to my homeopath appointment. The water was mid-thigh high so I had gotten off the pedal-vehicle to push as my headphones filled up with water, gargling the noise of my music.

There was a car in the road, pretty deep in water, with a frantic woman running around nearby. She was yelling with a half-closed throat, "My car! My car! Somebody help me with my car!"

I set my bike aside and got behind the little Volkswagen. She joined me in pushing it up into an elevated driveway, out of the flooded street. She never directly acknowledged my existence, continued to walk briskly around as she did before, stopping every few steps to change direction. I felt like I could hear her shallow breathing. She went into a stranger's house to use the telephone and I arrived a bit later at my appointment, soaking wet.

Wiener-Ass

A fifty-year-old bariatric surgeon who was also an MMA fighter came over and regularly got a thrill from instigating the little wiener dog. He was chasing the dog in circles around the house, room to room, and he tripped over himself. He instinctively barrel-rolled and ended in a fighting stance; a quick huff.

The dog got so flustered he released his anal glands. The smell of it filled the room and enveloped us individually. The surgeon's girlfriend scrunched her nose and had the brim of her shirt right up to her bottom eyelids. She slammed bleach wipes down in front of his face. She was convinced the butt juice was on the floor by the coffee table and was abruptly screeching at him to wipe it up.

The man was down in his hands and knees, normal-dog-sized level, and was scrubbing the floor as his girl yelled repeatedly with an itch in her throat, "Clean it! Clean it!" The dog had been sulking and had wandered all the way through the other room, toenails gently clicking on the hardwood floor.

Work

In my wicked insomnia days, living with a family sensitive to movement and noise, I would lie still and watch the cable-box clock change, one minute at a time. The blue light would whisper, and when the seven became an eight, the room seemed to illuminate in a bluer glow. I was thrilled when I was hired for a night-shift job, loading trucks— much less boredom.

I started working at United Parcel Service, eleven to four, in a large warehouse in Latham, NY. I was living with my infusion nurse at the time, and her two daughters. She let me use the car. Workboots, concrete and cardboard. People in brown clothes and trucks. Big metal chutes. I started loading tractor trailers during peak season, for Christmas. I'd get buried in packages, and dig myself out by stacking them. It felt like real-life Tetris.

This was around the time the paralysis came up through my torso— scaring me and making me question my physical diagnosis. I was going through neurologists like temporary mailmen. One hello, and then gone. The nerve tests were coming back slow, and I had been hospitalized for immobility, picked up off the side of the street. "Can you move your toes?" I just stared down at my feet, and they were so still.

So I medicated with stolen intravenous steroids, loads of Valium, Concerta and alcohol. I drank to be elevated, and to numb the pain. I took the ADHD medication to be able to stay active, and dilate my bloodstream. Valium I popped because it was there, it was offered to me, it was Valium.

I would get up from the couch, fall my way through the kitchen, drink whatever I could sneak, and trip my way over to the purse, or wherever the pills were. The little pink ones that kept me going. Stand up. Here I go, stable enough to not tip all the way over. I rolled blunts while I was driving, drinking right out of the bottles I kept in the car door. I'd pull off at a fork in the road before my workplace and get out of the car. I'd take my shirt off and smoke one to the face, thinking the shirt removal would prevent me from smelling like dank.

I'd show up to work, for safety huddle. Smoke was still coming out of my mouth. But I stopped smoking twenty minutes ago, can they see that? I stood normal. Like I was listening. Maybe it was cold enough to see my breath— but I couldn't see anyone else's.

I was numb-pain, so the location of my hands was very calculated, calibrated by experience. If I wore gloves my hands would be a different size, I wouldn't feel where they were, and I knew I would drop stuff. So I stacked and chucked packages with bare hands. I'd throw stuff up to land on top. I was an average-height female. My hands worn dry, they would crack and bleed. I had to hurry up. I'd slip down the ladder and wrap my bloody fingers in packing tape. My supervisor would watch me. "Be careful."

I was so tweaked out that I loaded faster than anyone in the whole warehouse, they said. One night they moved me to a different belt of trailers. "Show these guys how it's done." The drives home streaked by. I-87 to Albany, going 80mph, a figure was running fast, sprinting and keeping up next to the car. "It's not real, Leah, just keep driving." I did.

One night I blew right past the police station. Lights came on. I pulled to the side and rolled down the window. "Do you know why I pulled you over?" "No." "You don't?" He was startled. "You were going fifty in a thirty and you just ran that redlight." He pointed. "It was yellow when I went under it." "It was red." "I thought this was a forty-five." "You're in the city. In the city it's thirty miles an hour." "Oh." He asked me where I was coming from and if I had identification. I felt all around me with my arms. "I can't find it." "What about a work ID?" "The guy (my boss) keeps leaving it on his microwave." "Can you look at my finger?" I followed it with my eyes and asked him why I should, simultaneously. "You know what? Never mind, just go." Ok, I pulled off and went home, grateful since that would have been my third speeding ticket in a couple of weeks.

When I'd get home, I'd sneak inside, leaving my boots outside, they smelled so bad. I'd be burning with hunger, but didn't dare risk the crinkle of a wrapper or the crunch of a hard food. I'd hide food outside, in the old broken laundry dryer, but it'd freeze solid. No sleep and little food besides pills and alcohol ravaged my nervous system. I finally got a doctor who approved immunotherapy. I had to quit

42

my job. I had been one of the two people hired permanently out of the plethora of people hired for just the holiday season. With my infusions I wasn't supposed to over-exert myself, so I put in my resignation.

Paralyzed

I was having a backyard art show in the summer. It was a part of my fundraising efforts to raise money for a trip to Chicago to see a renowned neurologist. It was a silent auction, and we had a big donation-box. Art was hung from the clothesline and set up underneath canopies.

I had taken very naturally to dragging myself around on my knees, similar to the legless man from The Good, the Bad, and the Ugly. My legs were mostly paralyzed so I spent much of my time in a wheelchair. Many people came, including my piano teacher from when I was five. She had seen me in the paper and came to drop off a donation. She was a very nice, polite and kind woman. I since learned that she died of a heart-attack on the toilet at Walmart. She was found like that. She was mormon, and when I was a kid my mom would tell me "She's a very nice lady, but she's going to hell." Another man who read about my condition in the paper attended and had the same diagnosis as me. He pointed down. "It's like my legs aren't mine anymore."

With all the company I over-exerted myself and ended up in a slump. I could barely move. It started to rain. People gathered around me, in a circle. I had gotten soaked, and a friend of mine went inside to fetch me a dry shirt. "It's too scratchy." I spoke, since most fabrics hurt my skin. She graciously retrieved something softer and managed to redress me, out on the soggy ground.

They rolled me onto a blanket. The circle of people grabbed the edges, lifted and brought me inside, up the three claustrophobic steps into my room. I lied there crumpled up on my floor, with hoarse breathing. You could hear the scrape of every breath. "Do you want to go to the hospital?" My mom asked, speaking into my ear, crouched down to the floor. "Do you want to go to the hospital?" I could hear a smile in her voice and she stood up. "Come on, let's take her." My stepdad and stepbrother held me at each end and tossed me in the backseat.

Scene; emergency room. White, and I'm breathing every few chunks of seconds. "Look, she's not breathing!" my mom would say. "She's fine, she's fine, her oxygen is fine." A few minutes or maybe longer passed. There seemed to more of a bustle. I faded out. I imagined I was surrounded by clucking chickens. "You scared us there." A man was leaning over the railing of my bed. "We were gonna trache ya." My oxygen had dropped to thirty and they ended up dosing me with steroids. I came-to.

Neurology Appointment

I was wasted and it was my last neurology appointment before I left for Chicago for a potential clinical trial. I was waiting for a bus but ended up getting in a cab. I sorted out the wad of cash it would take to get to the doctor's office in Albany.

I talked and talked and talked to the cab driver, who probably had a mustache. When we arrived I felt all over and said "I can't find my money. Can I mail it to you?" He was like, "Uh, no." I found it under my leg.

In the appointment my doctor told me I had a misdiagnosis. "You know you're gonna get there and they're gonna tell you that you don't have this disease, right?" I know a single tear fell from my eye and he kept pressing me, asking me what was wrong. I don't recall what I said, but I know I included the statement "I'm sick of this shit."

I left the appointment and was in rough shape. I stood by the road alongside backed-up traffic. I looked at a tractor-trailer that had handles on the back to help workers climb up. I looked at a businessman in a sedan right behind it and motioned to the trailer's back end. He shrugged and lifted his hand, like, "Go ahead." I stepped on the back of the freight and rode it to the end of Wolf Road. Thank god it stopped at the light before pulling onto the thruway. I took the bus to Quail Street in Albany, and rode in a cab the rest of the way to my brother's apartment. I don't remember if I drank or took more pills there.

Wellbutrin

I couldn't sleep and all I could think to do was to see my old alcohol abuse

therapist. Who else did I have? I got there and described my circumstance. "I'm

going to have to refer you to the nurse practitioner, her office is right there next to

mine."

By the time I had an appointment it had been six months of persistent

insomnia. I articulated to her my hallucinations. "I'll walk by a mirror and be

covered in blood. When I look again it's gone. There's blood when I wash my hands

in the sink." I don't know what she thought of me. She never voiced her opinions or

observations. She wrote me a script for Risperdal.

I took the tiny pill, it being so small since it's often prescribed for small

children, and I slept for eight hours. I didn't care how weird it made me feel. I

hadn't slept more than a three-hour block in over six months. I thought I was going

to die of sleep-deprivation. But by the end of the first month medicated I was

heavy-set and terrified that I'd die if I went to sleep. I stopped taking it.

I had the hankerin' for some uppers and I arrived back at the nurse

practitioner. From all the sleep I had accumulated in a month a lot of my most

troubling hallucinations had dissipated. I told her I had ADHD. "What worked for

it?" I requested methylphenidate, an extended-release amphetamine. I mentioned I

had it off the street and it worked. She prescribed me Wellbutrin and said it would

work just as well.

My mom came outside. I was standing in the backyard gazing over at the graveyard beyond the fence. "What are you doing?" she asked.

"I'm waiting for it to kick in."

"Waiting for what to kick in?"

"Wellbutrin."

"What?! That's not going to *kick in,* that's like for quitting smoking."

I looked at her, squinting. "She told me it was a stimulant!"

"That bitch lied to you."

I went back to the nurse practitioner with a letter I wrote. It was something along the lines of "this is my life and I know what works for me." The only line I recall writing is "when I walk down the street I feel like the houses are going to eat me." That wasn't a lie. I remember that sensation vividly. I read the letter into the voicemail of my old english teacher so there was a communal aspect of my ocean of insanity.

The nurse practitioner prescribed it for me. 54mg ER; pink oblong tablet with 54 printed on one side. I took it a few times then started hoarding it. They eventually discharged me from the practice for forgetting to go for my ADHD medication. Now I actually had to get it off the streets.

Moon and River

I was drunk and unwell, and I decided to go to the dingy little coffee shop up the road where they played music. I faded in and out, and I think I got up there and started playing drums with the musicians. I ended up in the dust on the floor, unresponsive and in a weird set of convulsions where my back would arch, I couldn't open my eyes and my muscles were painfully contorted. I remember the blunt sound of my legs whacking against the chair and table legs as I was like a slug under salt on the floor.

My friends had to drag my body out by the shoulders and chuck my dead-weight rigor-mortis self into the back seat. They drove around because they didn't know how to get me home. They picked another friend of mine up off the street, and she must have sat next to the clump that was me. She knew where I lived and showed the other two where to bring me.

I of course lived in a locked building on the third floor at the end of the hall. Someone buzzed us in. I remember my two friends dropping me by the elevator, and a passerby looked down on us. I could feel it. Huffing, the girl who was holding my legs said, "Uh, uh, you're so heavy." The guy carrying me by the shoulders was a quiet type of guy, and probably didn't even want to leave the house that evening. At least I kept it interesting— or burdensome.

By the time they got me to the end of the hall I'm sure the two of them were past-done with me. They banged on the big metal door and a man named

Sunglasses opened it. "Oh, I got her, thanks." And he carried me inside. There was rambunctiousness in the apartment, they were drinking, too, and they placed me on the milk-crate of a futon. I slowly slid off of the side onto the floor and they moved me to the memory-foam bed in the dark. I heard my dad mumbling, probably hand to back of head, asking his roommate if she wanted me back in the living room to sleep. She replied in a yell, "She sleeps in there with me every goddamn night!" She settled back to quiet. "It's kind-of comforting."

My friend who had carried my legs called me a couple days later in a panic. "I just dropped you off! I don't even know what to!"

Flies

I was tripping on acid and making tea. I always resorted to simple ritualistic tasks when my mind and soul got off into a panic. The water was on the stove in a kettle and I was squinting to look at the fruit flies all over the cabinets. Our kitchen was infested. They were little, and black, and wiggly-walking all over the wooden swingy-doors of the boxes that held our dishes.

There were a slew of them that matched the color of the grains in the wood. They were more red-brown than black, with wings just the same. Oh my, they're dead, I thought. I got my face in too close of a vicinity to the tiny crunchy organisms, and one moved. AH!

I jolted the whole top half of my body back, and said "that's me!" I had been struggling with my health, with paralysis, breathing problems and idiopathic seizures. Who would want to put up with that for any given period of time, exacerbated of course by my behaviors and drug use. But I thought, that gross fruit-fly is me. It looks dead, and it's like *ew, gross.* Then it moves, and it's even more disturbing knowing that it's actually alive.

"Just make the tea, Leah. Just make the tea, and bring it to that girl. You're here, just be here."

Charlie

I recall staff at the community residence commenting on how gross it was to walk around the house barefoot. I used to walk around Mill Lane barefoot. My neighbor would call me "free-spirit" as I slapped my flat feet down the tiled hall to get my laundry. He said I reminded him of his girlfriend from decades ago.

"Will you buzz me in?!" He'd yell up to my third-story window I was often looking out of. A neighbor who lived in the same hall as me was yelling and hollering one day, because a girl was screaming and forcing herself into her apartment looking for Charlie. I tried to console the woman through the metal door once the girl left. I informed her that Charlie's apartment was in the same place, just on a different level, and that the girl must have been mistaken. I tried apologizing through the peephole but she kept calling me crazy white bitch and telling me to get away. She must have thought I was the same girl, despite my voice and demeanor. I think she was also on the phone, with the cops, begging for help.

When my friend told me the guy with the black car died, I was thinking it was some person whose Jetta had been towed a couple of days prior. When I realized it was Charlie, I saw the open investigation paperwork outside of his apartment. He had been dead for three days. That's where all the flies were coming from.

I saw that same girl who had been searching for Charlie walking up the sidewalk on State Street, looking drawn and a little dirty. It was right near where my cult met, and she stared and stared at me as she walked. She was barefoot, and carrying her sandals in one hand, by the straps.

Roses

It was one of those nights we were together and looking for something to do. I remember staring a guy down at Denny's and when he came over he had a tidbit of food on his lower face, in-between his lip and his chin. He was a little spaced-out and had a bag with him. Said he was waiting for five, six in the morning to go to some barracks or something.

We hit the road, headed for the rose garden. This was my idea. Gloves and a large trash bag crammed in the door of the car, we arrived. It was the middle of the night. You'd be surprised at the number of people that pass through the park at night. At least, I was. Walkers, runners, whole groups of people on bicycles with those little red blinkers and all. Every time we saw a person, we'd yell-whisper or say in a low-volume regular voice: *Person.* We'd drop flat on the ground and lie there until is was 'clear.'

Since we had one trash bag, we had to keep reconvening. My taller friend pulled up the brim of his shirt to make a pouch, and filled it up with roses. It was dark, but I could see it so clearly. *"Leah, look how many roses I got!"* as he tripped over his own foot and they all went flying. He jostled the broken flowers, but that was the happiest I've ever seen him in the brief history of our lives.

We filled that little car with roses, and the fragrance permeated the vehicle so strongly that it almost covered up the scent of body odor. We covered my nurse's front lawn in roses, entirely. We went back for more.

This trip, we each had a grocery bag; much more efficient. We had scissors, but rather, we tore the petalled plants off of their original bodies. We filled our bags, I don't know how many. "Person," the taller one said ever-so-calmly, but more stern this time. When I looked I saw the silhouette of a figure mid-air, leaping over a hedge in our direction- drawstrings flung upward with the flow of the jump. He hit the ground running— I could hear it - and instantly we booked it in three different directions. We were no longer a group. The silhouette was subliminally fast, but wouldn't catch us. None of us let go of a flower, not one.

Grit

I still imagine myself getting into accidents when riding in a car. I jokingly imagine myself getting bashed by a car when I'm walking, imitating the sounds of my bones crunching with onomatopoeia. But riding in the car sometimes I get legitimate tightness that speaks "This is it."

I remember that day I was randomly driving through Troy as it began raining. I had been in a Stewart's that I just left out of anxiety, with a woman saying "Oh, be careful, there are storms a comin'!" I'm like frantic, naturally, and don't care about the rain as far as inhibition goes, so I shrugged animately in silence and left to drive in my car. I was cruising down the hill towards a large 3-way intersection and my breaks didn't catch, at all. I was like, *oh,* as the line of stopped cars came closer to mine. I swerved off the road, like I had in many videogames over the course of my life, and slipped up a hill between a telephone pole and a tree. My breaks caught on the gravel, or the rough dirt, whatever it was, and the car stopped just a few feet before a solid tree. I felt all over my body quickly with my hands, ripped my phone and its cord and shoved it under my seat, because of white girl stigma of being on phones. I ran out of my car and down the gritty hill to the road, to the woman whose minivan I ricocheted off of. "Are you okay?" I asked her. She was incredibly nonchalant, and said that yes, she was okay, and I was lucky I stopped. She pointed up to the retaining wall that held the woods and dirt up. "If you went any farther you'd nosedive into the intersection." She was right. I hadn't even noticed.

My side mirror had flown off, and I dented the woman's bumper, but she said it was fine, since no one got hurt. She had asked if I was speeding, and I really wasn't. I was going about 32mph, but that's too fast for stopped traffic on a hill so steep they need a wall to keep the dirt from tumbling down.

When the cops came, they were looking around. "Where's your car?" Then one man looked up towards the sky and said, "Oh, *there's* your car." One guy went up and guided my car out as I reversed down the hill. It was a tight fit. They were like "Damn that's some good driving." They thought it was insane, and the woman officer just hoped my brakes worked so I didn't back into the police vehicle on the road. They didn't issue me a ticket. They said to go home, and get my brakes fixed. I asked about the woman whose car I hit, and they said she had gone home. She informed me before she had only just left work early because her daughter was afraid of thunderstorms.

Neverness

I worked at a Denny's in Schenectady, NY. I wore a bib-apron, a name-tag, a greasy black shirt. I felt like I was in a costume.

Overnights were tough, and those are what I worked ninety-percent of the time. Drunk people, high people, angry and vomiting. I was thankful when they fell asleep in the booths. I had recently quit doing drugs cold-turkey and joined a cult. Everybody at work said I was really weird. I'd stay up late talking to the cook and he kept saying "drugs make you real weird, make you act really weird. Dey mess you up." I was quiet about it. I really wasn't active in drug-use, I was just the palpable residue of my lifestyles.

I was always either working or running around with the ministry I was involved with. I was homeless, sleep-deprived and hallucinating. Slightly brainwashed, I saw demons in everything. They were in the children, and spoke through the adults. They chased me out of the kitchen and ran directly at me in the restaurant. I had an agreement with the bosses that I could go outside and run really fast around the block so that my legs wouldn't give out. I had to outrun the creatures that were after me. Overwhelmed, I would roll silverware and run around, sweating outside.

I was in trouble with the shelter I lived in for being out and about all the time. I didn't understand why or even that they wanted me to stay home at all. I quickly got kicked out for missing curfew, because I rode out to Rochester to pray for an already-deceased infant.

I slept in a couple cars and beds and then moved in with an older couple whose contract stated that I stay sober, and do what I'm supposed to do in life. Thinking about that dead baby I prayed for, I sat in a bar by myself and drank. So I was homeless again. I slept in various vehicles and other people's beds, the grease from work fermenting in each car I slept in. The aroma rose from the soles of my black shoes. A type of film had developed in the two pairs of pants that I owned. They were thick with grime. I couldn't even wash it out.

The songs at the restaurant played in a loop, and it reinforced my sense of insanity. I'd arrive and stand behind the counter, under the stinging fluorescent lights. The stocky little dishwasher with a lazy eye would come around the bend with a bin full of dishes. "It's like we nevva left." I started smoking weed with the cook. "I knew it!" The second dishwasher said to me. "I knew you did drugs!"

That same hyper dishwasher found me outside one day when I was coming in for a shift. I had opened my car door and just fell out. *No, not this.* I had been routinely paralyzed average four times a week but typically we'd just have prayer sessions and blame the demons. Groups of people would call out names of demons and pretend to fight them. Really I just had to wait for the episodes to be over.

The dishwasher came over to me with his high energy. "Woah." He picked me up and set me on the trunk of my Corolla. My manager came out and they both grabbed me under the pits and helped me inside. My legs were super-dragging. I sat in a booth and waited. My legs didn't seem to be coming back. My manager set me in a high-standing chair behind the kiosk where we took orders and welcomed customers. Lou happened to be there with a woman and tried not to feed the situation with too much attention or concern. "It's that thing?"

My arms were cramping, now, and my breathing was tense. I began to keel over. The overnight manager informed us that he was going home to curl up in bed and go to sleep. He left me at the computer up front and instructed the dishwasher to take orders. Dishwasher walked up to me quickly and tried to tell me what the customers asked for. "I told them I was batman." Smiling, he was, but I was nervous because this was only the beginning of the night and I knew that he had a short fuse. It was just him, my body, and the cook.

My friend came and picked me up, literally, and took me out. I seriously couldn't complete the job's duties that night. We left my car in the parking lot and I waited out my crumple on his couch. I wrote a thank-you letter to my bosses for the experience of working at Denny's. I didn't go back. When I informed another manager that I couldn't work a weekend he angrily hung up the phone.

Swarm

My friend asked me if I would help her clean out her fridge. I said sure. I did that type of thing for people all the time. Mind you, her power had been out for a month. They stole enough electricity to charge their phones with a long extension cord running up an alley to a neighbor's house. She hadn't thought to remove the food at all. It had sat there rotting, transforming, and growing mold.

The two-year-old opened the door of the refrigerator when I got there and a putrid smell wafted out. Putting her face in the bend of her arm the mother said "No, shut that!" as the boy did so and continued to run about the house. I stood very calmly still as the pungent fragrance hit me.

All the substances other than plastic within the appliance had turned to sludge. I don't recall one food item having an identity. I held open a contractor-sized garbage bag as my girl pulled bowls and infested containers from the shelves and dropped them in. She had to take breaks to gag and dry-heave.

They had turned the power back on, so when we got to the freezer up top the flies and the maggots were squirming in slow motion and frozen to the edges. I forgot to mention the flies. Perhaps a million, coating everything. She didn't have proper cleaning supplies but she had dish soap and we ripped an old bath towel into smaller pieces; rags. Half of the flies and maggots were adhering to the cold fibers of the towels shreds as we were wiping the freezer out. Touching hundreds of them was inevitable when I folded the towel over. The rag kept getting stuck to the inside

of the freezer like velcro. I don't know how I kept my cool. I had run out of power.

Goal-Oriented

I grew up in Schenectady and witnessed/heard about many of my friends' experiences in the treatment of mental health. Repeated inpatient stays, therapy that kicked up, obsessed over, and blamed the past. Camera-monitored rooms that consisted of a bed and a garbage can. Food stuffed with medications (that might have been paranoia) and groups with a drastic range of mental awarenesses.

When I was living with an older couple and "fighting demons" in a cult, they repeatedly told me that I needed mental help. I did, but was very resistant. Not just from hearsay, but from my personal endeavors of seeking out support.

One day I got so sick of hearing it and told the woman I lived with "Let me show you how the system works." We left for the hospital. She took me to Albany Medical Center's Emergency Department. I stated "I want to harm myself or others." They put me in blue clothes that had the consistency of a napkin. After many hours a doctor with an obnoxious tie and enthusiastic attitude said that I'd be going upstairs to their mental health unit. He left, and then two cute girls came in saying that I'd be going with them and the crazy doctor momentarily, and that I would be taken care of. They left and I didn't feel so bad. Then the mental police came. "You're going to CDPC." "What? They said I was going upstairs." "Nope, get your stuff." I got all of my belongings out of my zip-tied plastic box and went with them. I got in the police car that had "Mental" printed in the middle of the symbol. "What's CDPC?" "Capital District Psychiatric Center." It looked like a giant basement. It was large and flat, and made of cement.

There was a little woman in a dress who escorted me and you could tell she was forcing her flat affect. I went into a small room with her to fill out paperwork. I signed a sheet that said if I refused my medications they would inject them with a needle, restraining me if necessary. They put me in triage.

Triage was really a waiting room filled with chairs too heavy to lift, a long hallway attached with a designated men's bedroom, a women's bedroom, and two bathrooms with doors that had no latches. There were four beds in the women's bedroom. Mine was in the recess, hidden from the doorway but not the cameras. Everything was covered in plexiglass and we couldn't have pencils. There was a television set behind plexiglass, and nurses behind plexiglass, who were the only ones permitted to change the channel. There was a deck of playing cards consisting of about 36 cards, and the seven of diamonds had a bite mark out of it.

Most of the patients were over-medicated. The nurses didn't respond or make eye-contact. I sat in there for a week. Some guy kept barging into the women's bathroom while people were showering. He'd stand and bang on the plastic nurse's window for twenty minutes at a rip until they gave him a needle.

The couple I had been living with visited with pizza. I had been overmedicated by then. The husband said it was like I had been hit over the head with a brick. I was never admitted and never heard any word of such a thing. The wife came back and signed me out, told them I was sane. She was outraged by the conditions and called the senator. Nothing came of any of it.

A week or two later I ended up back in the same psych center, but for a very different reason. I had relapsed by drinking over the epitome of my life as a high-turnover waitress who went around with other mentally-ill people praying for frustrated families, the homeless, and dead babies. I drank for four days.

I'd chug beer and refill the bottles with mixed liquors. Pop the caps back on. I poured gin into all of my coffee, swerving to dodge the pedestrians on the narrow Guilderland roads. I'd get all pissed off, like it was their fault. But then there was that ever-growing ache in my heart. I was enrolled in a Catholic nursing school in Albany and drove to the college. I was obsessed with making movies so I was awkwardly filming the staff in their offices. I said I was making a project— a tour of the school. I got bored in between classes and drove to Schenectady to steal alcohol out of my dad's apartment. I legit said to myself that it didn't matter because he never got mad at me for eating anything out of the fridge. I figured Smirnoff counted. His whiskey wasn't as strong as mine, but it had to do. I couldn't even buy my own. I had no time, and I wasn't old enough. I got back to school, no recollection of paying the change it took to get through the tollbooth. My car apparently was parked very crooked. I very neatly wrote a whole english essay in a black-out. My resting place became the library.

I normally worked in the library for work-study and had befriended the librarians. I went in there and sat behind the check-out counter. The librarian supervising the library stood up and was looking at me. "You got this?" I swooped my hand and half-closed my eyes. "I got this." She left me in charge. Sitting there, I grimaced as I looked around. I felt like the students were looking at me, so I crawled beneath the librarian's desk. I fell asleep.

Next thing I saw was the friendly librarian's legs. She was wearing autumn-orange stockings and little brown shoes. I heard her comforting voice. "We're gonna need security." My vision swayed and I got up like a cat out of a nap. I crawled and stood up. "You don't have to do that." She said she thought it was best. I had been taken off campus to the hospital a few days prior for my legs giving out and me having severe confusion. That was before my relapse. Now, I was drunk, nicely telling the security officer that he didn't have to call the ambulance. He was my friend, too, I thought. I talked to him all the time. "Don't call the ambulance." But he was on the phone, and didn't stop. I became stern. "Don't call the ambulance." I got whiney and aggressive. I didn't want to get on the stretcher. "I'll end up in there for a week!" "No you won't." "Yes I will!" "Just go." "What, does this pink blanket mean I'm crazy?" I held up the edge of the fabric that was lying on the stretcher. They were trying to talk to me. Reason with me, maybe. I was blasted. I woke up in paper clothes. "No!"

All my personal belongings were zip-tied into a blue storage container on the floor. I felt so much more trapped, being there by accident this time. I couldn't do this again. I wanted so badly to leave, but I needed my phone and my keys. They were locked right beneath me. I was sitting on the container, always inching towards the exit, scooching on my ass. "Get back in there!" Suicide watch would snap at me. I imagined all the ways security would catch me if I ran. I wondered if they'd give me a shot in my ass. I was so hopeless.

Riding with the mental police, the same small woman asked why I was back so soon. "I was drunk." Someone somewhere told me that when I was blacked out I said the words "If I'm such a nuisance, just snowball me!" I was referring to the murderous technique of administering morphine until the patient is dead.

They had fabric blue clothes at CDPC, and my pants were too tight. The band squeezed my lower back, which was awful sensitive and affected my legs. I kept falling. I always tried to hold the band away from my back, so my hand was really down the back of my pants. They wouldn't give me a different size. We were all ordered to hide in a small room past a locked door, and I was crawling. "Get up!" I stood up and I fell. "Stop falling!" "That's why I was crawling!" I fell. "Stop falling, I'm too pregnant for this!" She really was extremely pregnant. I don't believe it was a safe environment for her to be working in. We all came in off the streets.

I was really trapped, this time. I was on my own. I started having DT's. My hands had strong tremors. I had severe chest pains and my neck was real tight. I didn't think it was the alcohol. I had only been drinking for four days. The nurses and a doctor observed me, and contemplated sending me back to the hospital, but gave me Ativan instead. Then a bunch of psych meds got piled on top of that. The Indian doctor came in my room and stuck his bare finger into my mouth. He felt around, to see if I had really swallowed the pills.

I couldn't sign myself out. It took two people with simultaneously-turned keys to open the door. There were no windows to open. No real air to breathe. The guy who would barge into the bathrooms from the last time was brought into the facility again. He smelled so bad, and there was no escaping it. The man working security went into the bathroom while the guy was showering and sprayed him with disinfectant-spray. The smelly guy earned the name "drip-drip" because whenever he had food or drink, he made a mess. At one point I saw him sit down where there was no chair. He fell to the ground on his ass and his kool-aid splashed everywhere.

I had to get out. I had been in another week. I knew I'd be stuck in there another week. I called my social-worker from highschool. We agreed that I could stay at her house until I found a rehab bed. She came and said I was sane, that I was safe. They let me go.

She took me to my mom's house for some reason. My mom told her not to take me because it would be enabling. So she dropped me at a women's shelter that was full. I fell and ripped my jeans on the carpet. It burned. My social-worker left and a shelter up the street was suggested to me. After a few knocks, they said they were full. The husband of the older couple I had lived with dropped off my car to me. I couldn't live with them because of my drinking, so I lived in my car.

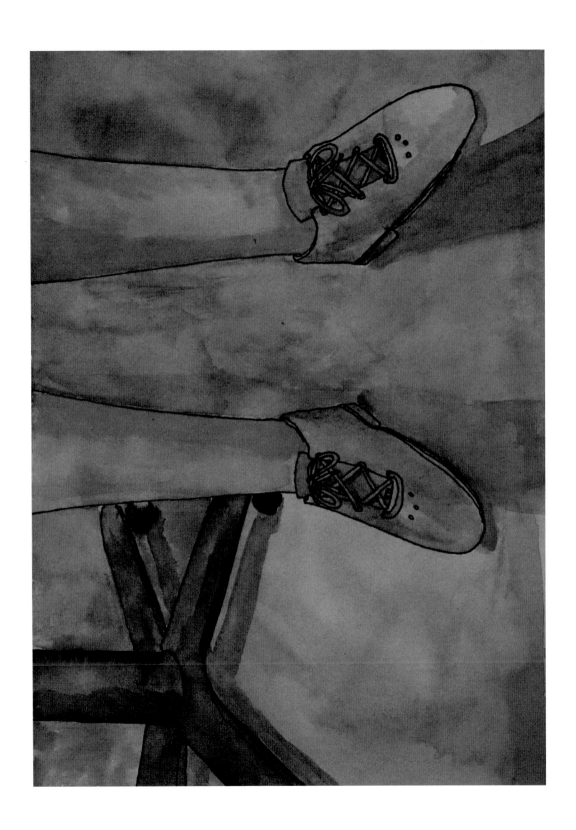

Houston,

My friend was a bad bulimic. I understood empathetically to an extent, her troubles. I was anorexic, myself, back in the day.

The first time I noticed she had an eating disorder was when we had pizza in a group setting that I wouldn't eat; my anxiety. She suggested that she might bring some home, but wouldn't eat any because she "just had mushrooms for dinner." Stick-thin, in high heels making her look longer, she wore a hat since she shaved half of her head in an adderal binge.

I would go to her house sporadically to sleep when I was homeless. I would mostly stop by to wash the dishes. She loathed dishes. I personally pictured it as evidence— proof of cooking, or even eating food. I hated them, too, when the dishes were my own. Sometimes she would pile the dishes in the bathtub; curtained so that she didn't have to look at them. Pots and pans, plates, glasses, silverware. We'd kneel down on a floor of towels and she'd put gloves on. We would clean and dry them all at once.

The active eating habits got really bad and her family was on to her. They wanted her to be well, in a sense. Really she would just get in trouble with them, and be on different terms as a result. So I went over one day to dye her hair and we flushed baking soda and vinegar in loads down the toilet. She said her family had somehow been removing buckets of partially digested food from the plumbing system, and she couldn't afford to be caught again.

After I had the plastic bonnet on her head, strands pulled through and dyed to create highlights, she went outside. I stood on the stoop as she crouched down to be at eye-level with the end of a PVC pipe that jutted out from the side of the foundation. "Houston, we have a problem," she uttered. Existing in the sunlight, the sight of it I remember was a sad soul trying to cope in the form of broccoli and bile, oozing out of the side of a house straight from the shitter.

Whiskey on the Bus

One day I must have been longing for companionship or something because I left the apartment to go see a friend. I went as I was, with nerve-damaged legs, black dress-pants, a hoodie. It was the middle of winter and I got on the bus, open glass of whiskey in my hand. Nothing said a word, and I didn't even think about it. The bus hummed on.

As I got off by the intersection to walk the rest of the way, it was dark and freezing cold. There were no sidewalks or streetlights and I thought my legs might give out a little too hard… I wasn't in good health. I stuck up my thumb. As cars zoomed by, some careening away when they saw me, one of them finally slowed down. *Yes,* I thought; *A ride.* Wait, oh, it's a cop. I must have looked around, at least with my shoulders as I stopped walking. I bent down and set my glass on the pavement in the shoulder of the road. I walked up to where the now-parked car was, in the nearest driveway.

"Someone called and said you were hitch-hiking," the first cop said. They asked where I was going and I told them. We all tried calling my friend; no answers. I didn't understand why they couldn't give me a ride, but I don't think I ever asked. The second cop was like, well we can't have you hitching. Look how dark it is out here, you could get hit by a car. I lifted my arms out a little, sideways. "I'd love to get hit by a car." He was like oh… The other cop grumbled words into his walkie that was clipped by his shoulder. "Now that you said that…" the second cop said, pivoting around and sighing with a tilt.

They said they'd have to take me to Albany Med. Which in turn meant Capital District Psychiatric Center. I grabbed the cop by the vest and shook him, wailing. "You don't understand! I can't go there!" As his head jostled on his neck and he looked at me with a look of a small child, he responded to me after I let go. "It's cold out, look at you, aren't you cold? Want to sit in the car while we work this out?" I sat with my legs dangling out of the side of the car, over the edge of the hard plastic seat. "Would you go to Ellis?" the walkie cop said. "Yeah." I knew I wouldn't be trapped there long.

They put me in the ER for acute intoxication. I was alright there at first, but then I started being a jerk. They begged me to just be calm, they were busy with real patients. I held myself around the railing of the bed and I cried. I ripped the discharge papers with my tense hands as I held them. The nurse threatened me with some form of hospital sentence then paused as she went to leave. "Are you withdrawing off of something else?" I said yes. Her demeanor changed, and I think she told me to hang in there. Lou came to get me and couldn't believe that I would cry so openly, in public. He would never make such a fool of himself. Little did he know, he made a fool of himself all the time with his words. That's why he was my friend.

Art

I used to volunteer at a local café, making simple meals and selling coffee. It was usually not populated at all, except for certain events; open mic's and poetry readings and cult meetings and such. I don't know what was going on this particular day, but there were quite a few people around, and I was just visiting. I sat at a table with an older calm man that I knew, who said he loved to oil paint just because of the smell, and the feeling of wiping the residue on his apron. I found that very impractical in my own life. I would just get paint freaking everywhere.

But a woman I knew came up to me and commented on my sobriety. I don't know if she had a stroke, and that's why she talked the way she did, but she held her heart monitor in her arms— which was really a Chihuahua. She told me to stay involved in the community, and that it was good that I was young and sober. I looked about me, more with my mind than my eyes. *I'm drunk right now.* I was twenty years old. The calm older man said that if I needed someone to talk to he was available. He had quit drinking an eon ago, when he was twenty-two. I thought that he wasn't a real alcoholic if he had quit that young. He hadn't even had the time to drink enough, I thought, to become addicted.

My Car

It was a Friday and I told my friend Sam I would bring her to work at two PM. That was the only thing on my agenda and it was mid-morning. I don't know where my flatmate was, but I was home alone. I checked the freezer— one pint of whiskey left. I thought to myself "that's not enough for the afternoon."

I was broke and underage and wouldn't settle that day for stealing beer or manipulating. So I crossed the living-room bed to the corner shelf and grabbed the furthest yellow sugar container. One never knew what would be inside one of them — they were all over the house. I had inspected every one. There was one in the kitchen that actually had sugar in it, but this one I opened up to reveal a bunch of sealed IV supplies. I picked a syringe and probably an 18-gauge needle and catheter. I've always had good veins. I sucked some whiskey right out of my early -morning glass and stuck it into the crook of my arm. I barely had to chase the vein.

I didn't expect it to really hit me, but it did, and fast. The blood dripped after I pulled the catheter out and it got all over the floor. The room moved a little and I grabbed the bleach. I quickly learned that ammonia works better. I was in a rush, and tidying up. I straightened up objects, made them parallel and perpendicular, parallel and perpendicular. I flipped my blanket-bed over to hide the blood droplets and put away the cleaning supplies. I didn't want the room to be askew— you know, just in case.

I poured the rest of the brown into a crinkly plastic bottle and the airbags went off. I didn't remember getting into the car, but I inched the windows down because of the smell. I pressed the tarpy bags down out of my face to reveal my smashed windshield. I was in the middle of an intersection around the corner from the apartment. I had to slip through the crack of how far my driver's door would open, because it had been bent. A woman with light shades on stared me down from inside of her car. Her whole fender was crumpled up and the car was very still. I squinted around and assumed to myself "Okay, nobody's dead." I couldn't get caught, not here, it was too close… too petty. I couldn't stop now. My car was unregistered. I bought the plates off ebay, and they were held on with duct tape and one screw each— that's how many I stuck in my underwear at Home Depot. I was very poor.

I got back in my car and sped off. There was a pursuit, I was later told, that was called off due to it being dangerous. Next thing I was aware of was maxing-out at 100mph in my 2004 Corolla and noticing a pick-up truck in the distance. I slowed down. I hit the brakes so hard the car swayed, and I still rear-ended him. Not hard, I thought. He gently pulled off the road as if to say "Let me get this young woman's insurance information." I kept driving.

My friend who used to be my drug counselor had a garage and lived two towns over. I thought: I'll move some stuff, park my car in there, shut the overhead and no one will find me. When I got there it was clear there was too much stuff to move. There was no way I was fitting a compact car in there. "Oo, a license-plate!" To me they were disposable and common. I picked up the pair and set to putting them on my car. You know, to be "incognito." I had still been drinking out of my water-bottle. I couldn't find my front plate so I just changed the back one. That's all you could see from the road anyway. My front bumper, what was left of it, was hanging under the front of my car. As I walked through the back porch I was hoping she hadn't moved the key, but the door was open.

"We were just talking about you." There was a man on my left, like "hi," and I looked and looked at the small figure on the couch ahead of me. It was her, but she was so small I almost thought she was her young daughter. When I realized that it was her and she was home, I briskly got on the couch and put her in my lap. "You're alive!"

I had walked in too fast for this to be my introduction to her fiancé, but I'm known for simply showing up as 'me.' "Did they follow you?" I don't think so. I had told them I got in an accident, and personally, I had honestly not seen a single cop the whole time.

"She has two different license plates on her car," thumb up over his shoulder, pair of scissors in the opposite hand. "Couldn't cut them, so I just tucked the airbags back in." I told them I found the plates in the garage and she said they were associated with her name because they came off of her car they had just totaled. "Oh, put mine back on!" I insisted. She had worked really hard for that car.

She told me she had just flatlined twice and gotten home from the hospital. I later felt responsible for that, because I cut her off most of her benzos when I stopped dealing. Now I didn't deal with anything. I had my phone shut off and lived in isolation because I was planning on killing myself. It was almost two.

I pointed at my watch's face. "I gotta go bring this bitch to work." I didn't remember her phone number and didn't have a phone, so I couldn't call. I didn't want to not show up, she hated that, and I didn't want to be unreliable. I was walking out the door when my ex-drug counselor asked me "Have you been drinking?" I didn't stop, just yelled out as the screen door was swinging behind me, "Nah, I quit drinking!"

My car was sliding like I was ending a donut-spin. Skidding to a stop, I was looking dead-ahead, both hands on the wheel. I saw some cars all over the place and a man in a dark long-sleeved shirt was running towards my vehicle. When he stopped outside my window he was shaking his hands like he was jazzing. *Different shirt, red hat, not a cop.* The car was in first and I kept checking. "No, no, no, you were just in a bad accident!" I had hit my head real hard off of the steering wheel and it was swelling up to the size of a soft-ball. I had no inkling at all that I hit my head, I thought I was just drunk. I blacked out very easily these days. My key was bent perpendicular somehow, but still in the ignition. I turned it and my car started. *That's it, it was just stalled.* The man was still at my window, beckoning "Don't, no, don't do that!" I drove and all the people that were scattered in the road split for me like the red sea.

I pulled up outside of Sam's boyfriend's house where she was staying, in the Historical District of Schenectady. "Just keep moving," I said to myself, "they won't know you're drunk." I skipped over the steps and up into the house. I was swinging my arm full circle. "Come on, gotta go to work!" I saw far more people than there actually were, but that didn't matter. She looked at me and said "I was just about to call you!" She got in the car. My corolla had no headlights at this point. My windshield was shattered. There was some of the body of the car left. "Are you okay with this?!" I was yelling over the music and the ringing in my ears, as I motioned across the whole car with my hand. "Yes," she said. I super-questioned and doubted reality. But I drove.

We kept talking, loud enough to understand over the grinding noise of this Chiddy-chiddy Bang-bang and the rap music. "Is this the way to Applebee's? I just can't remember…" My leftover whiskey was rolling around at her feet disguised as dirty spring water. She says I kept reaching over and touching her. I kept asking her if she was really there.

I was convinced that if I stopped for too long, the car would crap out and she wouldn't get to work on time. All of my effort would be vain. We were stopped at a redlight and a Glenville cop was sitting behind us. Sam explained that they weren't there for us; they had their turn signal on. "Okay, good." I must have already been convinced that I wasn't real anymore, that nobody could see me, because I pulled around the four cars ahead of us and ran the redlight. Everyone else started pulling over.

I was very content. My car was still running, and there was plenty of space for me to drive. I had both lanes to myself. I couldn't hear the sirens but I saw the police lights in my rearview mirror. I flopped my hand: "Don't worry, they're not for us." Sam was sitting very still. I remained evasive.

Somehow I was run onto a dead-end street by the airport, a couple of blocks from where Sam waitressed. The chief of police cut me off and I ran him into a ditch. He got out of his vehicle and stood in front of my car. I started revving the engine and he jumped behind a telephone pole. The whole town police force was parked behind me. They were yelling and came out with the guns. I looked at Sam and said, "I'm sorry, you might have to walk to work from here."

I got out of the car and quickly there was a gun right in my face. "Get the fuck on the ground!" They were screaming and hollering, and I didn't want my friend to see my brains blown out of my head, so I felt the cold asphalt touch my cheeks. That's the last solid sensation I remember ever having.

I had my hands up and the police were patting me down. They asked me what was in my pocket. A cop pulled a dummy I had made of myself out of the backseat of my car. I had a busted up car, a girl in a waitressing outfit, a dummy in a waitressing outfit, and I was fleeing from police. All the cop had to say, was, "What the fuck is going on?"

I had been planning on putting the dummy of myself, name-tag and outfit, in the parking lot of the Denny's where I used to work. I was going to run it over with my car and leave, have it covered with blood and all. Maybe that's where I was off to that morning. Gel food coloring makes the best fake blood, and that's what was in my pocket. They felt the lump and asked what it was. "Check yourself!" I yelled. If I reached for it, they'd shoot me, their guns were still aimed. If I said food coloring, it'd sound ridiculous. "What's in your pocket?" They asked again. "Check your fucking self!" Sam never made it to work.

The police had taken my shoes and cuffed my feet to my hands; I was kicking too much. Without limbs, I resorted to biting. I screamed at them that I had to die. The chief of police later told me that I screamed louder than any woman he had ever heard, for forty-five minutes straight, until they brought me to the hospital. In the station I had started with "Just bring Sam to work! Her life sucks! She doesn't have to know that! Just bring her to Applebee's!" I didn't know that she was standing right outside the holding cell, and could hear me. Eventually they told me they had brought her. Maybe they thought I'd calm down. I just resorted to screaming that I had to die— over, and over, and over.

I screamed at the officer that rode in the ambulance with me to the hospital. We argued and I bitched him out for being an asshole. At the hospital maybe eight cops wheeled me in. A nurse asked if they wanted me to be in the normal emergency room. "No! She's been kicking and biting police officers!" I do remember snapping at a cop with my teeth as he adjusted my restraints. He snatched his hands away and seethed.

The cops left the room and the hospital staff gave me a shot in my ass as I complained "I don't like needles!" I just didn't want to be controlled. I had to make a call. I only remembered two phone numbers. So I called my social worker from highschool. I went in numerical order. Nice. I never thought anything was a big deal. I don't know what I was even calling for, but she was at a football game for her son. I'm grateful. I called my friend Ashley second. She had helped me for a decade, a stable friendship, more on her end than mine. For some reason she showed up. I was still drunk, in my underwear, open gown. "Hey!" I probably hugged her. They had taken off my restraints before she got there. As the woman was unlatching a cuff, I brushed my head against her hand. "Did you just hug my hand with your face?" Yeah, mhm. The woman told Ashley that I was crazy when I came in, but "now she's an angel." She whispered in Ashley's ear, "We had to give her *huhmzhufm.*" mouth hidden behind a raise hand. "She just wouldn't calm down, and we had to give her a CAT scan." I instinctively started meowing. I was still oblivious to the fact that I had hit my head at all. I figured I was there for a mental evaluation, and that the cops were just waiting to pick me up. I said "Fuck you" to the doctor who suggested I might have a headache for a while. I thought he was making fun of me for having a future hangover.

I must have put my clothes back on, right? But in my memory I was hunched over in a hospital gown. I had swollen rings and bruises around my wrists from scrapping but I was walking away from the hospital room. Ashley said that she was told I was in the crazy ER only because the regular one was full. I kept looking around and rubbing my wrists as we left. *No cuffs?*

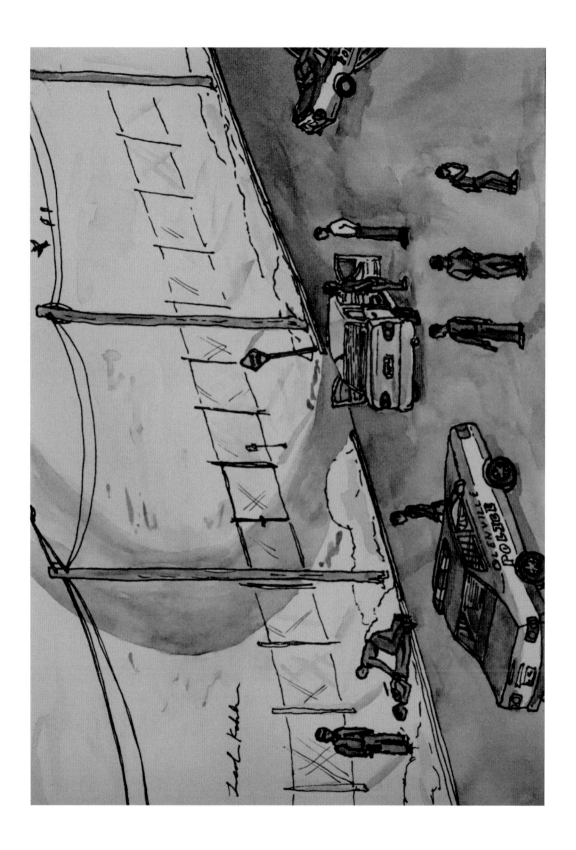

The Wheeled Chair

There was an abandoned YMCA behind the apartment I was living in. I crawled inside. They had an upper-level track, the kind that curved so fast it had banks. The floor was tilted up, lifted like the edges of a freshly opened burger wrapper.

I wanted to fly around that track, but with my nerves the way that they were (fucked), I knew that I wouldn't be able to run fast enough. But I got another idea when I saw there was a bicycle in the alley. If I made sure I could ride that bike, it might go fast enough for a thrill, or at least a break in the wind. I took it; brought it inside the apartment. I didn't have any spray paint to paint it a different color. By the looks of the last paint-job, it had certainly been stolen before. I held no remorse. It was just one of those bicycles that knew the exciting unstable life of often being stolen or repossessed. I coated it with a layer of black duct-tape.

The next day I rode it outside. It was a warmer winter day; the sun was out. I rode a couple of blocks pretty hard. That was a mistake. I either over-estimated the threshold of my body's capacity for physical exertion, or I was hoping I could push the envelope with that one. My legs went out on me. I lifted my leg from beneath the knee and placed my foot on the corresponding pedal. I got thrust forward with a swooping-jolting motion as my dead leg fell downward. I tried this again and again. *Come on, you stupid fucking legs.* I bumped into a telephone pole. I resorted to using the bike as a walker. I was perhaps five blocks from home.

My solid arms held my weight up against the handlebars and I dragged my legs; they scuffed behind. I made it to a benched bus stop under a bridge. This walker-guy from my old apartment building was sitting there. I wasn't a smoker, but I bummed a cigarette off of him, hoping it was laced or soaked in something. Last test-drag off him certainly wasn't just tobacco. This was just a cigarette. I smoked half and stuck the butt in one of the bicycle's pegs.

I made it up to the corner where there was a major 4-way intersection and a cement banister. I sat facing away from the street, away from the sun, on a cement block by a tree. My feet sat in mud, and squished about as I attempted to utilize my upper legs.

A woman in a coat and pajamas came by and accused me of smoking K2. "That's all I smoked!" I was pointing to the bicycle peg, my elbow locked. "It's a normal cigarette, try it and see." All the time I was squirming in a dire attempt to move my legs. I had been trying to stand up by holding on a tree branch, maybe that's why she stopped— the sheer sight of me. She lit up the last half of the cigarette and said she was calling the cops. I think she hugged me as she cried out about how she hated to see beautiful young girls doing this to themselves. The cops and EMT's arrived and the pajama lady whispered to them loud and clear. "I think she has a brain injury." I still had two black eyes from my car accident. I did have a headache real bad. The lady took the bicycle and said she had to go to the gym, but would store the bike for me. I had never met this woman but said OK. The bike was used to this sort of life.

A few minutes went by. I was concerned with nothing outside of my paralyzed legs. My feet were slathered in sunny mud from me twisting my upper half in hopes that my leg-nerves would reply. Some happy kid, my age or a little older, came up with the duct-taped bike. "Hey, isn't this yours? I saw you riding it earlier." The cops looked at me. "Yeah," my hand falling as I said it. "You can have it." "You sure?" "Yeah." He looked happier, still, than before. "Thanks!"

The emergency response team was talking about the bicycle, that hey, I could have sold it, gotten twenty bucks or something from the kid. "Yeah, I sorta thought about that." I had done worse things for twenty bucks. But I didn't care. "Whatever." I was saying don't bother... my legs don't even work.

They must have concluded that I ought to go to the hospital. Whether I smoked too many synthetics, had a TBI, or was a cripple on a bicycle, they couldn't leave me there on the side of the street, trying to avoid the sun I was sitting under. An officer picked me up, under the armpits, like a child. "Woah." I hadn't been picked up like that since I was a toddler. "Yeah, that's such-n-such. He's a brute." I apologized for getting mud all over and into the sheets on the stretcher. "It's fine," one said as another asked where the cameras were. "Is this for real? Is this real life?" As I looked straight up at the blue sky I wanted to say that dude, this is my life, every, single, day.

"Are you out running all over still?" My friend I ran cross country with was one of the EMT's. I motioned to my legs; "I can't." I don't remember her showing any acknowledgement. They put me in the ambulance.

The hospital. I was so sick of being in the hospital. I kept getting in trouble for wheeling about. "Stay in the waiting room." Even confined to that space in a wheelchair, I kept being chastised to sit still. A little girl had asked about my legs and if I'd been in a car accident. I said yes and went into no detail. Most people never understood that many of my issues were blatantly separate. I looked at the handicapped button for the automatic door. *I'm not in crisis. This isn't a lockdown.* I looked at a technician at her standing-computer. "It's downhill all the way home." She just smiled. I rolled over and pressed the button. As I was cruising out of the building an older woman was walking by, wind blowing in her hair. "Somebody's having fun!"

It was a long, single-laned street with parked cars and therefore no shoulders. The sidewalks were too busted-up but it really was downhill— such an incline that I maneuvered almost solely with the brakes. The chair rattled and a truck with the hospital's name printed on the side was stopped in traffic. He looked, but didn't move. The chair I was in still had the big bar over the top that kept people from folding it up or possibly stealing it. Then there's me.

The cars drove around me as I prayed. I made it to the bottom of the hill, and came to a round-a-bout. I sat there for a long time. Cars going around and around, I waited for my "in" but there didn't seem to be one. This would require boldness. I still couldn't use my legs. Some guy in a pick-up truck leaned out his window to wish me luck. I don't remember how I got through it. My brain must have blocked it out. The last thing I remember from there is the same ambulance driving by, EMT's staring, as if to say "Yo, didn't we just drop her off?"

There was fallen snow over the broken sidewalks so the furthest I could get was Stewart's. I remember sitting outside of the new liquor store and staring at it. But I wheeled over to the convenience store and pulled my ass out of the chair and into one of their seats. I texted Lou, asked him to pick me up at Stewart's, the one real close to home. He came inside and he saw me, saw the wheelchair, big bar up over the top. I slid into the wheelchair and he pushed me out. Someone we both knew was there, asking what happened and Lou just held up his hand, shook his head and continued walking. He crammed the chair with the bar into the back of his SUV. We went home.

I dragged myself up by the railing and I think Lou asked me something along the lines of "What the fuck." He suggested we switch rooms— livingroom for bedroom. He had given me the bedroom for "solace," which he happened to be in a lot of the time. His bed was in the livingroom to accommodate my "independence." The livingroom was a much larger space. "Since you keep coming home with large objects, like bicycles and wheelchairs." He thought I should have more room. I agreed and started packing my things. What he didn't know was that I was actually

packing to go to rehab.

Apple Cart

In rehab I sort-of deteriorated mentally. Well, I showed up freshly deteriorated. But my grasp on reality became diluted after maybe a month of being in the hospital wing. My brain was still active, but my awareness was botched, so my imagination and confusion took hold.

I had been with a roommate who was overmedicated on methadone, so we hallucinated together. I assured her that that was the right entrance, yes, and she was following invisible balls across the floor with her eyes, and her whole head. I would wear my clothes in the shower and pretend I was gardening in the rain, rearranging medical gloves that were ballooned up and tied full of water, which were really my crops.

I had another roommate who stated I'd just burst into song, any time of day or night. I recited rap music lyrics and begged to have some music. I screamed and groaned out of frustration and high levels of pain. I'd squirm and cry out all night, little did I know they could hear me throughout the whole unit. They started threatening to send me to the psych ward.

One day I jumped into bed and said "Let me know if the apples get here!" I was shocked that I had said it out loud and hoped no one had heard. By walks my overmedicated roommate, saying, "I'll go check." I had been hallucinating a man, grown, running down a sidewalk with a pulsating squeaky cart overflowing with apples. The guy was wearing a bonnet, and running full speed, apples tumbling off the cart as he went over the bumps of the walkway. I think my roommate really asked the staff if the apples had come up, yet. I don't think they knew how whacked we really were on the inside of our skulls.

Even when I had my own room and spent my days lying down, sweaty, in the dark, I'd mumble about the apples. I asked my nurse if she saw any, the order had just come in, I had seen the man slide pallets of apples under my bed. I leaned over the side of my hospital bed, and slid down until the crown of my head was resting on the floor. I looked under the bed and made eye-contact with the nurse, who was crawling around on the floor searching for the hidden apples. I started to laugh. My entirety had become thoroughly absurd.

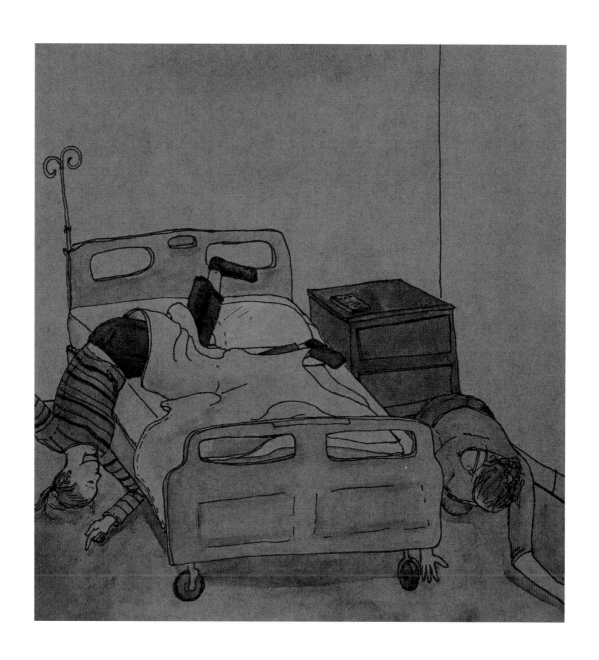

deliverance

"If she asks you if you can evacuate the house in under four minutes in case of a fire, just say *yes*. Don't tell them you'll drag yourself out on your ass if you're paralyzed, nothing like that." My counselor was telling me how to maneuver my screening, or interview, to get accepted into a mental health community residence. I had been in a 14 to 28 day rehab for over two months. The facility was resorting to placing me in a nursing home, otherwise I'd be dropped at a shelter. But then this woman came.

I was dressed as usual and was trying to decide whether to wash my hair again or not. The shampoo in the hospital wing where I resided was cheap and inconsistent. I wanted my hair to look healthy, but not too dried out and frizzy. The unit was so dry my counselor's voice would scratch with her vocal chords as soon as she walked into work. Everything was a static shock.

It was a shock to me that a program director would come to meet me. The last woman eyed my walker and said if I fell in the house they couldn't touch me-they'd call an EMT and I'd be discharged from the program.

I was on the floor in my room one night and asked for a cup of water. The woman who ran the rehab crouched down with a jingle of her keys and said "Leah, nobody's going to touch you with a ten-foot pole." My medical records were a real turn-off, having a neurological history. So they omitted my medical records and said it was all in my head.

I was taken out of group when my counselor gave me the spiel over the shoulder-height counter. It was a plea. I walked into an office with my potential adopter without a walking aid, as instructed. *My hair's too greasy. Shit.* "I can't sit because of my back and I have photosensitivity." I pointed up at the fluorescent light and kept my sunglasses resting on my face. "Can you get out of the house in four minutes?" Yes. "Can you cook?" Yes. "Are you a messy cook?" She told me about the program and that they go on "outings" on weekends, like to the arcade or the beach. "I've never been to the beach," I blurted. Of course I had. I was brain-damaged, and emitting sounds. She looked me up and down with her eyeballs, head resting on her fist held up by her elbow. *I failed.* I knew it. I just fucked it up.

I was going to a nursing home. Maybe an infirmary. I was crazy, and had been told I was a bit wetbrain during my inpatient stay. I came this far for more hell.

"Leah, she asked do you want to go to dinner at the house?"

Going Back Home

After I got out of rehab and was living at a community residence, I went back home to get my artwork. Lou was the older man I was living with. Him and I had converted the original living room to his bedroom, with his bed and all of that. His prior bedroom had become mine, me sleeping on a blanket on the floor and utilizing a round table for my artwork in the corner.

When I returned to get my things, I had been gone for two and a half months. There wasn't much inclination that I was returning. Lou himself said "I figured this would be the last time we spoke."

Yet my room was still there, with all my things, my dummy sitting in the wheelchair I stole from the hospital. The massage table was on the floor, flat, where my bed would be. There was a dummy lying on that, too. That's where the cat sleeps, he said. My coffee cup was on the shelf, still. The coffee was in a tiny dried up moldy puddle, solidified to the bottom of the mug. I stood there holding it. "Lou," I said. He looked at me, and then down, throwing his hands up in the air a little.

Schoolhouse Mouse

I was getting a head-start on community service hours even though it wasn't asked of me. I figured I ought to volunteer. I was in a community that was new to me, and this man I knew asked if I wanted to volunteer at a schoolhouse museum for a 101-year old woman I had read about in the paper. I was excited, I thought it would be an honor to meet this century-old woman and do a favor; a good deed.

The man drove me out to the museum, which was a small schoolhouse that maintained its antique features. My job was to sit in this classroom, and give tours when guests arrived. Tours of one room. I believe that in all the times I went, we had two families visit; parents, maybe a grandparent, couple of kids. I feel like all I did was say "This is a pencil from nineteen forty-two! Look at that lunchbox…" I was complimented on my intelligence but I think I was perceived as about twelve, like I was there with my father. Did I mention the man never left? We both just sat there and I felt more useless than normal.

I sat in a medium desk because there were various sizes, since all the grade-school kids used to share a room. The man persistently gossiped about people he wasn't supposed to mention by name, and I tried to read a book. He also kept commenting about a pesky mouse they had been trying to poison. I attempted to find solace in the bathroom. I needed something, anything. This was a gruesome way to be sober. I don't even hesitate, sometimes, to contemplate drinking bleach. Anything, to even feel sick; it would be a stronger sensation than this.

I returned to the regular room of course. I couldn't hide in the bathroom forever. But I also perused the janitorial closet, and I found that poor mouse. I thought I was hallucinating, or maybe that it was a very large bug. I caught it, as it was moving slow, and I picked it up. It was bleeding out of both ends, breathing fully— more fully than I ever have. I just kept holding it.

The man that brought me there didn't say much about it. His vibe emanated something like "Of course it's supposed to be poisoned." His eyes were asking me why I would hold it in my bare hands. I held it in the car all the way home, but I wasn't going home. I went to the blue bicycle shop that sold hoarded trinkets and bicycles/supplies. I kept suggesting putting it under the car tire to put it out of its suffering. We both knew it was dying. The driver just jutted his head back and forth, muttering "Ohm…" repeatedly. When I got out of the car he drove off before I could set the mouse on the ground.

My older friend was out there with no shirt, I'm sure, and bleached hair. I don't know how drunk he was, but he said he'd take care of the mouse. He'd stomp on it, he said, since I couldn't handle it. He really just buried the mouse alive.

A Book

It was November, in Upstate, NY. I had been diagnosed with mononucleosis, and man, did I feel it. The extreme fatigue, fevers and nausea. I was panicked about my direction in life and the constraint I felt I needed to have in order to keep things to myself. I wanted to force myself forward by hallucinogenically clearing my mind.

I went to Schenectady to cop some acid, and trip, then save some for my home environment. I took four tabs the first night. I had my friend hold my outer layer of clothes, in the park, at night, because I was overheating. "You have everything? You got my string?" I kept asking her, making sure, and she got louder and more abrupt as she kept confirming: "Yes. I've got it. Don't worry." She walked and swung her arms at angles interchangeably.

By the time we got back to her house, someone was after her. We slipped into the house and glided into the back room, where we abruptly stopped in the dark. Her mom answered the door and confirmed that her daughter wasn't home. We spoke in whispers as the woman persistently drove around the block and stalked us through the bedroom window. It was supposedly over $35 and something about a mailbox. We had to walk to the bank. It was an endless trek. I had been overheating, so I left the house in my T-shirt and short-shorts. After a little bit of walking I grabbed my friend's arm and shuddered. "Your teeth are chattering! *something-something about a jacket.*"

I'm not going back, is what I exclaimed. I was standing like a stick, tense, pale, and all fucked up. "I made a decision. I'm sticking to it!" I trembled in the cold for what, the two miles, down to the glow of an ATM in the dead of downtown Schenectady, whatever time it was.

At some point another kid entered the picture. He was a kid I recognized from highschool that I knew in passing; striped shirts, backwards hats, skateboard. He would often wave in greeting. He looked scruffier, now. Not in the hair, really, but in the skin almost.

We all ended up wandering. The girl really had lost my string, and I was potentially obsessed with finding it, because she insisted it wasn't gone. My string was really a pristine-white shoelace I got from a convict in rehab. I used it as a belt. We walked and walked and walked, looking through the muddy, sifty, frosty leaves. I looked for that lace for hours. I was exhausted. My tendons were stretched around my bones like ratchet straps. I stopped, standing atop a stone wall. The trees were moving like large creatures around me; we coexisted. My friend kept complaining, saying that drugs didn't work, and she didn't know why people kept doing them. I had just previously witnessed her put all nine remaining tabs into her mouth. I also witnessed her sitting on a counter— open bread bags all over— eyes wide like subway tunnels, choke down a jar of psilocybin mushroom-honey.

At some point we made it back to the yard, then we were within the walls of the bedroom that I had hidden in hours earlier. We lied on the floor since there was no bed. I had made her roll up the air mattress earlier that was flat, deflated; ripped. I was like "It's taking up so much space." Skinny guy would slowly walk by the room and mumble *"popped mah damn air mattress,"* shaking his head. He also wore a backwards hat.

The girl hugged like a fridge; rigid and cold. I got up. I re-entered the room and the scruffy kid looked up at me. "Mom?"

Standing in the darkness, pants sagging, relieved by the lack of harsh light, penetrating noise and conversation, I looked down at the heap of hoarded clothes that had no known origin. Everything so solemnly colorless, I realized I had everything I needed. Spine being torn apart by strychnine, held still, I knew I had all my memories. I had myself; fragmented or not. I didn't need no shoelace to write no book.

The Cab Drive

A mini-van, yellow, with a grinding noise and the back latch rusted open. "It's cooler in here, but I don't think the cops'll like that." The driver motioned to the back with a move of his head and a look in the rearview mirror. I looked back, it was wide-open and free— a tunnel to the outside, and I didn't even fantasize about tumbling out.

At the Sunoco I looped a tiny red strand of elastic through the rusted latch and taped it shut with electrical tape. It stayed shut the 48 miles home. He bought me gas station coffee, and he had no teeth. He was five months clean from crack and kept turning down the rock music to give me advice. He informed me of the practice of holding on with little goals in mind, like getting dentures and not having to admit he relapsed. He told me that to get A's in college, all I have to do is go to class, and do the homework. Never miss a math class. He commented on how he loved that time of morning, early, peaceful, and better with the blanket of clouds because the sun wasn't in his eyes. I could understand what he was saying. He said drinking alcohol is overrated, stick with the marijuana, and leave the crack alone. He stated that he thought he outlived his addiction— that it had lost its appeal. He told me how in Dallas he snorted coke at the bar, and within two weeks he was cooking up and smoking crack. He smoked rock for thirty-six years. "Y'ain't missin' nothin'." He motioned his hand forward in a circle by his head. "Play the tape through."

Towels

I asked my psychiatrist if one could overdose on Buspar. She tilted her head at a bit of an angle, leaning backward, and said "Well, you can overdose on any medication. Why do you ask?"

She was about to prescribe that one to me.

"I was just curious," I said, and explained how a story of someone needing their stomach pumped just flashed through my mind.

When I think of overdoses, substances like cocaine and heroin come to mind. But what's more familiar to me, personally, is that sensation that hits, tall and dense, and I know for a fact that I have taken too much.

One of the most minor things I ever took too much of was an amino acid derived from green tea. I wasn't supposed to take more than four chewables in a day, and I knew that. Two to three times a week, yeah, I got it. The bottle's half-gone, and there are six, maybe seven redbull cans hidden behind my closet door. My heart is steadily beating, but I'm severely questioning if this is reality.

I move slow, through this vision that just might be life. The wood floor stays still, nice and laminated, and I lean my carcass to look down the corridor. It's dark, some later time of night, when it's quiet in a community residence for the mentally unwell. I move toward the light.

Okay, my heart is pumping faster, now. I've seeped into the darkness. I get to the edge of a wall by the laundry-room. "Ashley?" I muster up-and-out at the woman shifting side-to-side, violently folding towels.

Cigs

I was not conscientious of Halloween this particular year. I was attending a mental health program and I had been taking acid all week. My spine felt deteriorated and ripped. I walked slowly, the hall twisting in a wavy vortex. The carpets creeped up the walls and the offices were all open, yet seemingly vacant. I saw no souls.

I looked with my head held straight and my eyes focused downward. I'd suck in air, and eventually sigh it out. The bugs were comforting me, ever-present beneath my skin. It was halloween or something, because everyone was dressed up. The people with intellectual disability and psychological torment swarmed in this large area referred to as the kitchen. I was slow-moving and deep-breathing, for survival through the pain, and a counselor touched my shoulder in passing. "You alright, Leah?" My downward-facing eyes were open wide. My breath and stillness was my only response. My nerves were being separated from themselves, in a hard fight, like a microscopic gruesome battle. At least that's what it felt like. I was being torn apart.

"Aaagggghhhh, I have to go home." I was lying horizontal on a bench in the smoke-shed outside, where everyone smoked cigarettes, communed around two dirty buckets. "Your pain's not real." Another counselor said, flicking her cigarette as she didn't even look at me. I was holding my leg up, foot propped against the wall, to alleviate some of the pressure on my sacral area. There was still this treatment telling me I was never ill, never paralyzed, never in real pain… The term conversion disorder that came from rehab emanated in the counselors' minds and I questioned my sanity. This disorder is a physical manifestation of mental trauma. A literal translation of "It's all in your head." I kept falling and the psychiatrist, when asked about conversion disorder, told me "It will work itself out." My knees suffered and I dragged myself, sometimes. Wondering if my life had even been real.

I went back inside to stick it out and the costumes weren't costumes anymore. There was a woman made out of peacocks, and a skeleton smoking a cigarette. I went on, keeping my eyes glued to the ever-squirming floor. Was my whole life just a trip? And when would it be over?

Empathetic

There's this woman that allowed me space. Overwhelmed I normally was, she'd sit and endure me. My pacing. My frantic complaints.

She dwelled in a large office, during business hours. Filled with her, her desk, aisles of filing cabinets and nine ceiling light fixtures, the space accommodated my rambunctious spirit. I'd show up and she'd sit calmly, the environment seemingly laced with every pace of mine.

Nothing seemed to bother her, but on the inside it probably did. By the time I calmed down, after a year or so, she admitted it out of the side of her mouth. "Remember when you used to pace? I was like *oh* my *god.*"

I showed up high on molly once. I was quite frustrated and paranoid. I knelt on the floor over and over again, changing position. The whole time I didn't loosen the grip I had on the skin about my torso— except to readjust, of course. "When was the last time you slept?" I acted like I was counting. "Friday" or something. I believe it was two days prior. I think she assumed it was just my unmedicated bipolar disorder. I'm a very honest person. I just get extremely nervous, and paranoid, around my relapses. I hide them, plan them, hover over them like treasures. Eventually I would break down and admit. I first apologized for my condition that day and how I acted. "You were very tense." She held her arms up from her shoulders at right-angles. I was suggested a sleep journal. I flushed the rest of my drugs and kept the act hidden for three or four months. I told her it was a relapse as I was standing behind her and touching her hair. "I'm not mad at you."

Someone I volunteered with was driving me home and I asked them if I could "stop by the office." That's all I said. I entered and told the woman that I wasn't stressed. I sat in her lap and let out breath. My shoulders dropped and she uttered "You just relaxed! I felt it!"

Whoops

I went to an amusement park with the mental health program people. Went swimming, rode the slides. My friend I was with said he threw up in his mouth on the first ride. He began to lay low.

I ended up with my war-vet friend following me around. We went on a twisting and swinging and turning clamp-in machine. He tensed up almost immediately. By the middle of it he was yelling, nearly foaming at the mouth. "This is why I never jumped out of a fucking plane in the service! This is why I never jumped out of a fucking plane in the fucking service!" I honestly don't know if he was in a foreign war, but I know he was a native veteran of alcoholism, injury and pain. As the ride slowed to a stop he was taking big breaths. He apologized to the younger kids beside him for swearing.

As we walked on, we met up with a staff member or two. I took some ibuprofen out of a sandwich-bag full. Everything gave me a headache. My friend was now calm and kept partaking in the torture. "Well, you already got me to go on that ride." He'd do it again, and he did. Ride after ride, he endured. It showed me that I could endure my own anxiety.

We got to a roller coaster, the kind that consisted of a single loop— it was power-launch, went 'round and around. We went on, him, I, and a staff member. I sat towards the back and saw him lock up as it started; tighter than the seats' clamps. Upside-down his body lifted off the seat and his hat he had tucked under his leg went flying. All the coins fell out of his pockets. His possessions reigned free, and after, he asked the ride attendant about his hat. It had flown over the fence.

There were sensors en route to the hat, and the park workers refused to temporarily shut down the ride to retrieve the cap. He was really attached to that hat; kept mentioning it. He had gotten it on a trip they took to the zoo earlier in the year. It was already faded from wearing it so much. Some guy in a vest said they'd collect it after the park closed and mail it to his home address. I hopped the fence.

The ride we just left automatically shut down, since I passed by a sensor. A man came to escort me out of the park. I didn't care, I had already concluded that that hat meant more to my friend than any park-ride shut-down meant to anybody. The security officer said that he felt bad, he didn't like escorting nice, good people out of the park. He knew I was just helping my friend. But he didn't know what I knew; I'm not a good person.

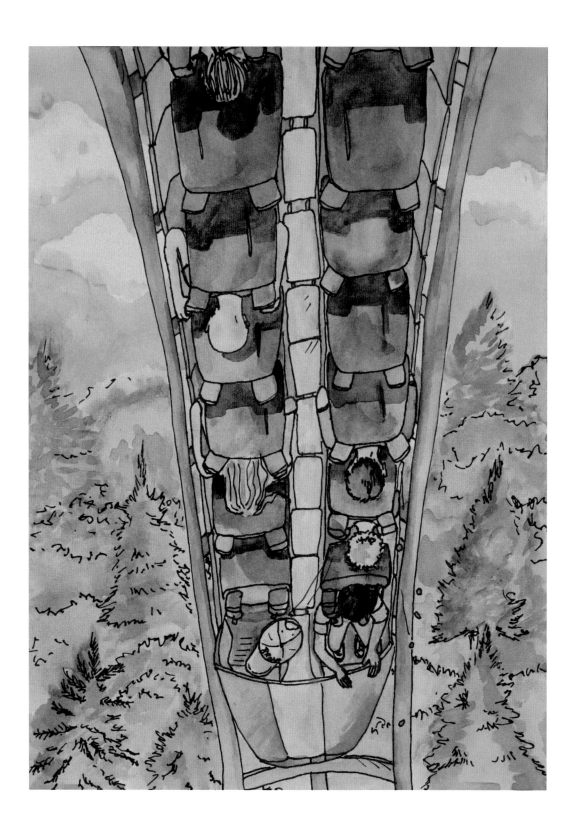

Couch Broke up a Marriage

At dog training I was asked to go up to the stage with the puppy and demonstrate. I was standing on the floor, of course, and the puppy, on the stage.

"I can't see," I said, and handed the trainer my glasses. I looked down at half a dog. "I still can't see." But I tried. I only had about 25 percent of my vision, on the far left; practically some inflated peripheral; on one side. I didn't feel totally in my skin. I'm sure it was just a migraine.

The dog was full, and over working for treats. We just sort of stood there. "I'm sorry, I'm distracted," I mentioned. We traded, glasses for puppy. "It's hard with twenty eyes on you," she said as she handed the prescription eyewear to me. I didn't even think about the eyes; I couldn't feel them. I felt more crowded by the furniture. There were like a hundred chairs in that room. Honestly, I appreciate an audience. I often find I'm just talking to myself, and that feels nearly fruitless. I was just overheated and confused by my sensory input. I couldn't see.

I am oddly intimidated by furniture. It broke up a marriage. I remember when this couple was moving into an apartment, and the couch got wedged in the doorway between two rooms. It was a little too big for the passageway. The woman was on one side, yelling, "Bring it around! Bring it around!" The silent sufferers on the other side kept pushing anyways, cramming it worse and worse, tighter and tighter like a doorstop. It was gouging the wooden doorframe with snug little crevices. Everyone had been bitching all day.

The man and the woman who were separated by a couch had been engaged and had been planning/buying things for the wedding. The man left with his son who had been shoving alongside of him. He never went back. I imagine that couch, still wedged there.

I Haven't Seen Him Since the Flood

"What's your favorite past-time?" "Me?" "Yeah, you. Leah." "Throwing dummies off buildings." "You're the best."

I don't know how to describe him specifically, but he was like a needy puppy. Almost seeming lost, but knowing what he was doing, he craved approval of some sort. Honestly, though, I think often all we're looking for is comfort.

I had been put on a mood stabilizer by my psychiatrist. I finally agreed to taking a medication since I had been "spinning [my] wheels for what, eighteen months?" I was in a mental health program I signed myself into. Where else did I have to turn? I was more than hesitant to take medications, for almost all of the times I went on bipolar meds or anti-depressants, it ended badly. I was allergic to many substances I had tried for mental health, believe it or not. My cells are just as sensitive as me. I went on a newer pharmaceutical this time. I kept asking if I would get fat. "This is not a weight gainer," she tried to assure me.

The insurance approval lapsed and I was a slight wreck about it. I finally agreed to take a medicine and the preauthorization wasn't submitted in time. Usually it was me messing with my pills. I missed a shift at the animal shelter and I stood in the rain more-or-less crying, just like the frozen sky, for an hour. The road was a thick sheet of ice, which is why the bus didn't come. Corporate compliance for the halfway house came and picked up my miserable ass from my apartment. Everyone was running late because of the weather. She dropped me off at the mental health program where I could get a hold of my psychiatrist. I'm better in-person.

One of the counselors was standing right outside of the door. "You can't go in! It's closed, we're closed." "My meds! I don't have my meds!" I was walking across the ice at normal-weather speed. "Alright, come in." She swooped her hair down and around with her head in a movement to open the door.

The maintenance girl insisted that her day was worse than mine. "I've been here since 6am!" I sat in the common area and watched all of the staff scurry. It was raining, inside, on the first floor of a three-story commercial building. All the ice on the roof was melting and invading the structure as water.

I went back and forth with my therapist who had her hair tied up and kept looking down, to the side, and smiling. How human she looked. "I'll call you when I hear from doc." At one point, standing under the stairs, I was telling her stories, and as she motioned that she had to leave I said OK. I slapped my arms around her in a hug. "Oh," she said. I always hugged her too hard because 90% of the time I was just looking at her and holding it in. I'd hugged her a couple of times before and she'd stumble. "Be careful."

The puppy-like guy I introduced earlier was in a T-shirt, wearing a smile. He said something about everybody working together to move stuff out from under the massive leaks. "Yeah, it's like a team-building exercise." He looked at me probably squinting behind his tinted glasses— I could see the lift in his cheeks— "I know. It's nice, isn't it?" He released the squint. "And I still don't like 'em."

When I was sitting next to the rain I was mentioning my med-change in staccato, and the big puppy leaned over. "Between you and me…" he looked side to side, hands resting on the back of a chair supporting more weight than his legs. "Doc put me on Anthrax." "What? What'd she put you on?" That couldn't be right. "She put me on Anthrax."

I Forget to Turn the Lights on Then Stumble Around in the Dark

I'm in a LeSabre Custom by Buick. There's a hole where the window adjuster should be. I trace the curvature of the inside of the car with my eyes— but not my mind's eye. My knee aches and has cute little shooting pains along the cap from all the times I've fallen.

I wish I could describe to you my experience. The ache is from my burning snow-soaked toes up through my tingling hands that write this. My migraine has been combatted with a tiny PEZ-looking pill. I want to look at the driver, I even have my shades on, but I won't. I just listen to the grunge of his voice. He offered me a paper cup of Pepsi. It has a lid but he still holds it in place when we go around corners.

My neck is strained from falling hard on the ice. My spine's the whole of me. The passenger behind me says "holy firetruck" about the weather but now he's saying fuck every other word. I have a jab in the left of my head and it smells like old french fries. I'm tolerating the country music easily; that's different. They talked about Metro PCS and I got a flashback to one of my favorite posters of a goofy-looking guy with arms crossed like "Ah got uh phone!" Nice grin and tilt.

I thought we were about three miles closer to my destination than we were so I had put this writing away. It would have been too embarrassing to take it back out after the struggle it took for me to put it away in my rummage of a bookbag. I crammed it behind a box of macaroni and cheese I don't remember putting in there. At some point I caught a glimpse of the cab driver's dirty teeth.

When I got to the house I picked up dog poop and couldn't find the garbage cans. I put the trash outside in the snow, snuggled up against a wall. When I got into the garage and found the pails, I smacked a rectangle in three designated spots because I didn't know if it was a button, a light, or a garage-door opener. I was startled when it clicked and the overhead started to move. The light is on. Did I turn that on? When I went in the basement I thought a coat was a live person. I held my sternum.

Made in the USA
Coppell, TX
29 October 2023

23572488R00088